Beyond a World Divided

Beyond
A WORLD
DIVIDED

Human Values in
the Brain-Mind Science
of Roger Sperry

ERIKA ERDMANN
AND DAVID STOVER

Foreword by David H. Hubel

SHAMBHALA
Boston & London
1991

Shambhala Publications, Inc.
Horticultural Hall
300 Massachusetts Avenue
Boston, Massachusetts 02115

Shambhala Publications, Inc.
Random Century House
20 Vauxhall Bridge Road
London SW1V 2SA

9 8 7 6 5 4 3 2 1

First Edition

Printed in the United States of America on acid-free paper

Distributed in the United States by Random House, Inc.,
in Canada by Random House of Canada Ltd, and in the
United Kingdom by the Random Century Group

Library of Congress Cataloging-in-Publication Data

Erdmann, Erika.
    Beyond a world divided: human values in the brain-
mind science of Roger Sperry/Erika Erdmann and David
Stover; foreword by David H. Hubel.
        p.   cm.
    Includes bibliographical references.
    ISBN 0-87773-590-5
    1. Consciousness.   2. Sperry, Roger, 1913–   .
    3. Mind-brain identity theory.   4. Split brain.
    5. Religion and science.   I. Stover, David.   II. Title.
QP411.E73   1991   90-53376
612.8'2—dc20   CIP

Our minds are concerned with the future while our hearts appreciate the present. We therefore dedicate this book both to all our planet's far-sighted, responsible, future-oriented thinkers and to those who shaped our lives in ways immeasurable, large and small; in particular,

to Karl H. Erdmann   to Susan Worley

—E.E.   —D.S.

Contents

CONTENTS

Contents

Foreword

My first exposure to Roger Sperry was in the fall of 1963, when I heard him speak at the international Physiological Congress in Montreal. This was my first scientific congress. I had just begun my training in clinical neurology, and I had not yet done any research. Sperry's talk was a revelation. It is hard today to recapture our state of knowledge of the nervous system in the early fifties, a time when the brain was widely regarded as a highly plastic slate on which the environment wrote its message. In his talk Sperry described an experiment to see how long it would take for the nervous system of a cat to relearn the proper use of muscles after the extensor and effector tendons had been interchanged. The relearning never took place; the brain was not nearly as malleable as we had thought. This experiment was characteristic of the simplicity and lucidity of all of Sperry's work on development during that era.

My next encounter with Roger Sperry was again indirect; I found myself, two years later, in the army and posted to Walter Reed Army Institute of Research, sharing a suite of laboratory cubicles with Ronald Myers, who had just got his Ph.D. under Sperry at the University of Chicago. Myers's thesis involved the corpus callosum in cats. Up to that time, no one had any idea of the function of this huge bundle of nerve fibers. But, by asking characteristically simple questions and obtaining characteristically clean answers, Sperry and Myers provided clear proof that the corpus callosum transmitted knowledge from one hemisphere of the brain to the opposite one. Two simple and beautiful papers in the journal *Brain* in 1965 and 1967 report about the first such studies on humans, who had their corpus callosum surgically interrupted to reduce severe and intractable epilepsy. The second of these papers is a vivid example of the possibility of coming to grips experimentally with the problems of mind and consciousness.

Much of this book deals with Sperry's refusal to accept the premise that natural phenomena occurring at one level of complexity can be explained in terms of phenomena occurring at antecedent levels. It is admittedly necessary to know something about the lower-level phenomena in order to proceed to the next stage of complexity, but that alone is not sufficient. As anyone who grew up in the fifties knows, the subject of neural circuits was impossible to understand until one knew about impulses, synaptic transmissions, excitation, and inhibition. But to understand the circuits it has been necessary to discover how the elements are put together, using the tools of anatomy and physiology. Is it possible that the study of mental processes represents a still higher level, bearing the same relation to circuits as the circuits bear to single-cell ionic mechanisms? My feeling is that we still know too little about the mind, in physiological terms, to predict.

We have many tantalizing fragments, however. One can perhaps think of these fragments as the beginning of a higher-order knowledge that is based on brain circuits but that cannot be deduced from them. Perhaps because my main research is brain circuits, my prejudice is that circuits may go a long way toward understanding mind and consciousness. We can be reasonably optimistic about understanding bat sonar and birdsong in the near future. My instincts, for what they are worth, suggest to me that we have to take seriously E. O. Wilson's ideas that things like altruism and the human tendency to superstitions and religious beliefs are in some sense genetically determined and so probably dependent on brain circuits, and understandable in those terms. (Of course the details of such beliefs must be learned, just as the alphabet is.) The trouble is that we still know too little about brain circuits, and far too little about mentation, to have much confidence in our prejudices!

I find it hard to deal with words like *mind*. When we use it in everyday life we surely know what we mean. But when we proceed to investigate the mind scientifically we immediately realize how little we know about it. The little we do know, such as the fact that it can be split, has already changed the way we think about it, just as our attitude to the word *sky* has been changed by the work of astronomers. The notion of "understanding the mind" is a hard one to pin down because someday, as a result of scientific studies, the word *mind* will have come to connote something better defined and qualitatively different. We may then wisely keep the word *mind*, with all its present richness and fuzziness, for everyday use and substitute a new word for scientific purposes, just as astronomers speak of the *universe* and we keep the *sky* for everyday use.

Sperry takes the conceptualization a step further, insisting that the hierarchy is not a one-way street in which higher-level processes arise passively out of lower ones. The higher levels exert effects back on the lower levels; consciousness is seen as capable of affecting brain circuits, for example. To grasp Sperry's reasoning, it may be helpful to trace it from the first instance in which it was publicly expressed—at the first conference of the Central Nervous System and Behavior, held in the United States in 1958. During the discussion Sperry stated that the stimuli used for conditioning must, if they are to work, involve subjective experience. That is, the animal must "feel" the punishment and "taste" the reward. In short, Sperry widens his focus to include the entire animal he studies. Elaborations of this point of view in later papers all depend on a constantly widening focus, of which this book tells the story.

In my introduction to *Two Hemispheres—One Brain: Functions of the Corpus Callosum* (1986) I wrote that Roger Sperry "originated a different way of thinking about consciousness" that may have

an impact similar to that of the revolution of thought initiated
by Copernicus and Darwin. I have not changed my mind about
this statement.

David H. Hubel

Preface

This book examines the contributions of Nobel Prize–winning neuroscientist Roger Sperry to the bridging of the chasm between facts and values—the great divide between opposing worldviews that impedes humanity's progress toward a safe and secure future.

The work presents the first discussion of Sperry's ideas aimed not at the neuroscientist or philosopher but at the general reader. We have chosen his thoughts in that area not because we are unaware of those of others but because we believe that his insights into the mind-brain relationship are of key relevance to the fact-value controversy.

The first part of the book, "The Dilemma," describes the contrast—and its dangers—between the worldview of science and that of religion.

The second part, "The Quest," examines Sperry's proposed solution to the problem: a view of reality that integrates facts and values into a natural hierarchy. With the emergence of consciousness, thought, and foresight, evaluative directives for action can no longer be excluded from our view of the world. Sperry was led to his concern with values through his pioneering research in the field of brain development and right-left hemisphere differences in the brain—which we briefly treat to lend weight to his theories—and his probing quest into the nature and impact of consciousness. We also describe his battles through criticism and rejection and show that he has—in spite of arguments to the contrary based upon misconceptions of his thoughts—never left the solid fundamentals of science.

In the third part of the book, "The Hope," six scientists speak out on his behalf, and anxiety from the side of religion is calmed. The theory of evolution is explained not as an enemy of faith but as the source of religious experience. If that experience can be disengaged from its clinging to supernatural powers and attached to our fragile and endangered biosphere, we will be able to look with renewed hope into the future.

No longer adrift, carried by forces beyond our control toward an unknown fate that may include degradation or extinction, our thoughts permit us to steer toward one consciously perceived highest goal: the enhancement of the quality of existence with a perspective of responsibility that includes our descendants and the web of living-nonliving interrelations on earth.

We have chosen Sperry's philosophical contributions for discussion, not because we are unaware of those of other persons, but because we believe that his insights into the mind-brain relationship are of key relevance to the fact-value controversy— and to the future of humanity itself. In addition, our special experiences allow us to interpret correctly, and clearly, the significance of work that has frequently been misunderstood and misinterpreted.

You may wonder why we introduce our main topic relatively late in the book—only after a scenario and discussion of "the dilemma" confronting us. In the course of Sperry's psychobiology classes at the California Institute of Technology, it became clear that his ideas were far more easily grasped when presented after, rather than before, a discussion of the warring worldviews of science and religion, facts and values, which now divide humanity. To appreciate Sperry's answer to them, the depth and complexity of the problems and questions facing us must first be fully understood.

But there is still a more important question to tackle. Why is a thorough understanding of the mind-brain relation of such relevance to the fate of our species? The answer to this query will occupy most of the pages that follow. But we will stake out our ground from the start.

Our thoughts, attitudes, and values determine our behavior, the fate of humankind, the fate of our earth. Some scientists, especially some sociobiologists, see values as genetically determined, brain-bound, and unchangeable. Religionists hold that values were given to us by supernatural powers and are eternal, sacred, and unchangeable. Hard-line behaviorists dismiss values as irrelevant. We believe that none of these three conceptions is adequate. With unchanged values in a changing world, we cannot survive. With values conceived as irrelevant, life is shorn of all meaning. How, then, can we find values that are solid, but not unchangeable; sacred, but not immovable? We look at the problem first from the perspective of traditional science, then from the perspective of traditional religion, and finally from Sperry's new perspective. And there we find common ground and new hope.

This book is the result of several years' work, through three countries, one ocean, and through innumerable drafts. It began its life as a master's thesis by Erika Erdmann. When she decided to seek book publication for the work, David Stover, a long-time friend and correspondent, became involved in the project, first as an interested reader, then as coauthor. (We might note that the two of us had never met in person until work on the book was well underway!) The material has been reworked many times over the past several years, so that at times even we have trouble telling who contributed this phrase or that.

Both of us share a concern for the future. Erika Erdmann, the book's senior author, believes that the philosophical ideas of Roger Sperry present great hope for a bright and fulfilling future, but only if (1) his thoughts and ideas on *emergent causation* are understood and interpreted not as opposed to, but as compatible with, modern science; (2) his conception of the *forward thrust of evolution* is understood and interpreted not as a blind rush for power but as a constant search for new constellations of creative relationships, like those that have preceded the emergence of every new supervening whole in nature; and (3) the immense difficulty of the way ahead is clearly recognized, and any step in the desired direction by any concerned person is fully supported.

For his part, David Stover believes that the ideas we will discuss in the following pages may present one (if not the only) way out of our current dilemma, and that such ideas deserve to be brought to, and discussed by, a wider audience beyond the scientific and philosophical communities. That, of course, is our intent here.

Both of us believe that the closing of the deep chasm between opposing worldviews—concern with facts at the expense of values as contrasted with concern with values at the expense of facts—must become our first priority. Both of us, but especially Stover, would have liked to examine other and related approaches to the problems of human—and humane—survival; but we decided to opt for a narrower but more focused approach.

Even so, it is impossible to deal with a topic as encompassing as this without error, for which we accept full responsibility. We also expect, and invite, criticism.

Acknowledgments

We both are grateful to Dr. Thomas Natsoulas for providing us with a synopsis of his refutation of Sperry's critics.

We wish to thank our editor at Shambhala, Dr. Jeremy Hayward, who provided valuable suggestions for improving the work, and who opened our eyes to a new way of thinking and strengthened our belief that a merging of objective assessment and subjective experience will lead to further inspirations advancing humanity.

We wish to express our gratitude to the many other individuals who contributed in ways large and small but always meaningful, only a few of whom could be mentioned here.

We have drawn on the work of many thinkers and philosophers in writing *Beyond a World Divided,* most notably Roger Sperry; but we hasten to add that, unless otherwise noted, the opinions expressed and conclusions drawn are ours alone.

The first-person plural pronoun *we* is used throughout, except where personal experiences of the senior author with Dr. Sperry are discussed.

I am grateful to my husband, Karl H. Erdmann, for his confidence in my abilities, for his constant support, and for his patience with my absentmindedness.

I wish to thank Dr. Frank Cardelle, my M.A.-thesis mentor from Columbia Pacific University, for his counsel: "Don't be too academic; put your heart into it."

A word of appreciation is due, also, to my might-have-been

ACKNOWLEDGMENTS

coauthor, Sandra Tsing Loh, and to Mrs. Norma Sperry for reading the entire manuscript and making valuable suggestions for improvement. Furthermore, I wish to express sincere gratitude to Mrs. Sperry for her warm hospitality.

Most of all, I wish to thank Professor R. W. Sperry for providing my life with a new content.

Only rarely is an individual able to achieve a new perspective, a new view of the world—one which dissolves irreconcilable contrasts and casts problems in a new light. Even rarer are the few who appeal to human emotion without recourse to the occult and supernatural—and with a logical consistency that remains free of cold detachment and cynicism.

I have been fortunate to know such a person and will share with you what I can of his work, his struggle, and his thoughts.

Erika Erdmann

I wish to thank my wife, Susan Worley, for her love, her support—and her patience.

David Stover

Part 1

THE DILEMMA

· 1 ·
The Rift

We are walking with complacency into a situation more ominous than any
in recent history, . . . worse than any the human race has ever known.
—C. P. Snow

The earth trembled under the feet of stampeding beasts. Eyes
crazed with fear, tusks covered with foam, trunks flailing, the
animals raced on. Thunder numbed their senses, and the wild
yells of their pursuers and the smoke of the hunters' fires confused them even more. Every experience hammered into their
brains the need to race faster—faster—faster—

The gorge! The leader reared, trying to turn, to stem the on-
rush of hundreds of tons of panicked flesh—to no avail. One
last lunatic look and he was thrust into the ravine.

Wave after wave of the huge mammals surged forward and
vanished.

The time was thirty thousand years ago. The place was Spain.
The hunters were our ancestors.

The time is now. Grey masses are still stampeding toward the
abyss. But we are not the hunters anymore. We are the hunted.
The hunters are our ill-adjusted values.

Why do the forces driving us lead to such frenzied confusion?

A rift, or cleavage, runs through our conception of reality,
separating from its fundaments the most vital aspect of nature.
Religious persons call this most vital aspect the human soul.
Others refer to it as mind or spirit. No matter what its name, it
is the highest, most advanced product of biological evolution—

at least the highest product of which we are aware. Yet there are many who deny the natural, evolutionary origin of the mind or soul. They denounce evolution as evil and misguided, and assign the soul to a far different world—a dual world in which matter and mind are separate realms. A leading Christian revivalist's vigorous attacks against evolution, against science, and against logic itself contain the hope that "the material-energy-chance world view can be rolled back with all its results across all of life."[1]

From the world attacked, the enormously successful world of numbers, measurements, and objective fact—science—the hopelessness of the cleavage is confirmed.

"Conscience has no observable referent . . . and is therefore meaningless," says defender of logical positivism Burnham Beckwith,[2] and "the noun '*right*' cannot be directly or indirectly defined by pointing."[3] Therefore "political science should merely aid men to do what they already want to do and . . . the problem of whether what they want to do is ethical is nonsensical."[4]

Such pronouncements make science a headless monster and provide fuel for revivalist Francis Schaeffer's conclusion that "there is no way to mix these two total world views. They are separate entities that cannot be synthesized."[5]

The greatest threat arises from the fact that both worlds aspire to a monopoly of truth; they both attempt to engulf the other.

Not only science and religion but all human endeavor is divided by this rift. The division shows itself most dangerously in politics where, to defend ideologies often unsupported by fact, weapons are being devised that could destroy not only our species but the earth's entire life support system.

What is this rift that divides and threatens our world? In its broadest sense, the gap runs between those who defend values at the expense of facts and those who put objective facts ahead of human values. Although preoccupation with short-term concerns veils the threat for most people, its presence and its danger are clearly perceived by farsighted and independently thinking persons.

Speaking at the end of a life dedicated to the study of human action in history, Arnold Toynbee saw our future imperiled by a combination of overpopulation, greed, and anarchy in international affairs. He warned such a combination will, if complacency postpones our option to make responsible decisions too long, lead to a sudden realization of imminent disaster.

> I suspect that a worldwide totalitarian movement of the communist-fascist kind may overthrow existing institutions—such as local sovereignty, political democracy, economic private enterprise—and that at the eleventh hour some such totalitarian movement will stabilize human affairs by taking drastic actions in which indispensable fundamental reforms will be intertwined with atrocious acts of injustice.[6]

Toynbee's thorough knowledge of history permitted him to discern not only the risk of the total destruction of mankind but also the probability of a desperate last-minute solution if complacency prevailed too long. Our choice of life over death and the kind of life we choose depends first of all upon the triumph of our ingenuity over our complacency.

Another person able to penetrate the veil, Norman Cousins, called "a spokesman for the human race" by an interviewer, spoke with equal concern, though in a lighter manner.

> First, I would want to call attention to the fact that we are living in a very primitive age in human history. Despite all the apparent evidences of civilization, we are really bumping along at a very low level and dealing primarily with philosophies that point us away from survival. . . . We are left with the need to devise a collective mechanism for survival. We've tried in the past to evolve such mechanisms, but they haven't kept pace with certain other aspects of human development: our fascination with weaponry, for example, or our ability to devise means for destroying large numbers of people. We have, you see, no corresponding advance in terms of our philosophy or ideology.[7]

Albert Einstein, again, was more serious.

> All our lauded technological progress—our very civilization—is
> like the ax in the hand of a pathological criminal.[8]

All three of these visionaries agree about the gravity of the
threat to our species and our earth—the stranglehold of the
ideas and ideals that threaten to destroy us. The dangers facing
us are real. Yet all of them are man-made. Neither supernatural
deities nor irreversible laws of history hold us in thrall. Nor are
we slaves of rigid genetic determinism. Though burdened with
an ancient heritage of an increasingly fierce struggle for power,
we are yet blessed with minds capable of insight, wisdom, concern, and foresight. Our salvation does not lie in rolling back
our knowledge and insight; it lies in their advance.

Advance in human knowledge generally involves widening
our perspective to account for facts and observations that were
previously unexplainable. For instance, in 450 B.C.E., the Greek
historian Herodotus recorded reports of sailors who said that,
as they ventured farther and farther down the coast of Africa,
they eventually observed the high noon sun to their north, not
to the south. "I do not believe it," Herodotus said cautiously of
the tale, "but I write it down here nonetheless. Maybe someone
else will believe it." Today, of course, we *do* believe the sailors'
account, because our view of the world has changed since the
time of Herodotus—from an image of a flat region surrounding
the Mediterranean to one of a globe suspended in space.

Similarly, for decades the ancient Egyptians tried without
success, using the most complicated calculations, to bring the
newly invented calendar, which was based on observations of
the sky, into accord with the traditional calendar, based on the
flooding of the Nile. It was all to no avail, until it occurred to
some genius that, perhaps, the sun and the stars were more
accurate timekeepers than the river's floods.

Such enlargements of man's worldview have taken place
throughout history. Once the earth was the center of the uni-

verse, with the sun revolving around it. Before evolutionary theory was developed, biologists thought of species as fixed and unchanging. Before Einstein devised the theory of relativity, Newton's laws of motion reigned supreme. In each case, it was never nature that changed, only our perception of it; and in each case, the new and more realistic perception depended on a larger, more encompassing perspective. That wider perspective allowed us to account for facts previously thought inexplicable and to do things once thought impossible.

Clearly, human survival depends upon yet another widening of our perspective, yet another enlargement of our worldview, or, as the historian of science Thomas Kuhn would put it, yet another shift of paradigm. Will it be possible to arrive at a new perception of nature that goes beyond the worldviews of science and religion, recognizing the necessity of both for human survival, yet also admitting the insufficiency of each alone? Will it be possible to integrate both into a single harmonious view of the universe, one belief system which violates neither man's craving for logical consistency nor the need for emotional satisfaction and spiritual elevation? Will it be possible to bridge the deadly chasm which prevents us from communicating and cooperating with one another?

It is true that valiant efforts to attain these goals have already been made. Why did they fail? Why does it seem impossible to counter the momentum of humankind's headlong rush into oblivion? It is because we are trapped in just those patterns of thought that have created the chasm. Therefore, new conceptions, based on new insights, are needed.

The present work deals with such new conceptions and insights: the confusion and controversy they have aroused, their battles through criticism, their partial success, and their immense promise for our future.

In exploring these new insights, we will keep three key questions in mind.

1. Is it possible to disengage ourselves from the compelling but contradictory systems of belief that threaten to destroy us?

2. Can we discover or create the new, more comprehensive understanding or worldview we so desperately need?
3. Will we be able to attach our allegiance to this new and unifying worldview?

Let us explore these issues together. But first, let us sharpen the focus on our divided world.

·2·
A World Divided

Modern science has existed for less than one-tenth of recorded history. Yet in barely four hundred years, science has transformed both the world and our view of the world. The universe inhabited by medieval Europeans was extremely limited in space and time. At its center was the earth, created only a few thousand years before by supernatural means, destined to endure only a short while more until the dawning of Judgment Day. The stars and planets were no more than lights in the sky created for man's benefit. Indeed, by modern standards *limited* seems hardly an adequate description of the medieval universe: *claustrophobic* might be better.

Science changed all that. Men like Copernicus and Galileo challenged the orthodoxy of Aristotle and the Church. Observation and experimentation revealed a universe that was far larger and more complex than the scholars of the Middle Ages had ever dreamed. The horizons of time and space began to recede at breathtaking speed. Twentieth-century science has revealed a universe immense beyond imagination, complex beyond comprehension; a universe, in the words of the British geneticist J. B. S. Haldane, that is not only "queerer than we imagine, but queerer than we can imagine."

But the promise of science is this: though there are still many things we do not understand about the universe, the scientific method offers a tested and time-proven way of attacking and unraveling these mysteries. As long as scientists continue to work, the sum total of human knowledge continues to grow. Last year's puzzle becomes this year's breakthrough, which becomes next year's textbook dogma. No other pattern or process of thought rivals science in producing new and useful knowledge about the world we live in.

The benefits of science have been enormous, both in increasing our understanding of the universe and in increasing our control over the physical world. But nothing is without a price, and there are many in the world today who feel that the price paid for the success of science has been too high: in exchange for empirical knowledge—and the wealth and power derived from that knowledge—science has taken from us our very souls.

Science's pursuit of "hard," "cold," "objective" knowledge has robbed human life of its warmth, its beauty, its subjective meaning. Science has destroyed the old myths which gave us comfort and cannot provide a suitable substitute. Humanity has been left alone in a vast uncaring universe—a speck of life stranded on a dust mote afloat on a sea of space, without purpose, without hope.

What a contrast, these critics of science would say, between the world of science and that of religion. Religion can offer mankind meaning; it affirms the importance of human values and human experience; it provides comfort and solace and purpose.

There is only one problem, proponents of science reply. Religion offers comfort at the expense of truth. Religionists turn away from the unpleasant realities revealed by science, to seek relief in made-up myths and fairy stories.

Thus the battle lines are set; thus the world is divided. This division is most fatal where rigid dogmatism decries tolerance and open-mindedness, where a deep cleavage exists between the world of the mind and the world of matter, and where "man" and "nature" are experienced as fundamentally different. This is the world we will examine most closely, for here the danger is greatest. There are areas of human thought—process theology, for instance, and certain Eastern religions—where attempts to reconcile science and religion have been made, often quite successfully. We are not ignorant of these efforts; but at the same time we feel we must concentrate on those areas where the chasm is deepest and the threat to the species' survival most pressing.

The Worldview of Science

> The ancient covenant is in pieces; man at last knows that he is alone in the unfeeling immensity of the universe out of which he emerged only by chance. —Jacques Monod

Despite the enormous influence science exerts in the world today, most people remain unfamiliar with how science operates or with what it can tell us about the world. When we think of science at all, we tend to think of its products: miracle drugs, nuclear reactors, expeditions to the moon.

To better understand the conflict between science and religion—between the realm of facts and that of values—we need to understand science itself better. And one of the best places to gain insight into the world of the hard sciences is in the book *Chance and Necessity* by the French microbiologist and Nobel laureate Jacques Monod.[1]

Central to the scientific worldview is the attempt to understand reality by reducing complex wholes to more easily grasped parts. Instead of trying to understand how an entire organism works, we concentrate, rather, on specific aspects or parts of that organism: on the functioning of certain organs, or the workings of a single cell, or the complicated structure of the genes within the nucleus of that cell.

This process is called *reductionism*. We hasten to point out that there is nothing wrong with reductionism as such. Much of the success of modern science occurred because of this approach. The world is too complex to be understood when taken all in one piece, so to speak; the trail of causes and effects is too tangled for even the best and brightest to make sense of. As with criminology, the key to success in science is to narrow the field of investigation, to isolate the facts that are salient from those that are not.

But it is important to differentiate between *methodological* and *epistemological* reductionism. Arthur Peacocke explains that methodological reduction, dismantling a complex whole into its constituents, is a prerequisite for research and understanding and is not controversial.[2] Epistemological reductionism, on the other hand, claims that theories which are suitable for more complex systems may be freely translated into theories suitable for lower levels of the natural hierarchy. Thus, when we feel and enjoy the warmth of a summer day, what is actually happening is "nothing but" the excitation of certain neurons in our brain by the rapid motion of molecules. Such epistemological reduction is controversial with good reason: it often generates ontological reduction, that is, the reduction of the entire rich and complex world of subjective experience into essentially meaningless components and the draining out of our lives of all meaning, love, and joy.

This kind of reductionism is dangerous. It ignores all those properties of the whole that come into being only through the specific relationship of one part to another. What is left is something entirely different from the item we initially began to examine. A frog, for instance, ceases to be a frog if we know nothing about it but the structural details of its individual cells. To be sure, it is important to know the details of that cell structure in order to better understand frog physiology; but cell structure is not the whole story. The frog is more than merely the sum of its cells. The whole is more than the sum of its parts, and there are aspects of reality to which we will remain forever blind if we study only the cells, not the frog as a whole (or, for that matter, only the frog, and not the ecosystem of which it is part).

The more we narrow our focus the more information is lost, so that as each part in isolation is reduced to its individual components, still another set of holistic properties disappears from the "reality" we are describing, until what is finally left—what physicists recognize as the *ultimate basis of reality*—no longer bears even the remotest resemblance to the world as we know it.

As long as reductionism is seen for what it is—a useful but limited tool in our exploration of the universe—there is no problem. The difficulty is that the reductionists are in the habit of reconstructing the entire world from the entities in their particular field of study, leaving out of consideration all the emergent properties that make nature as complex as it is—and that lend human life its richness and meaning.

For instance: Monod is convinced that the nature of life, even human life, can be fully explained in terms of the materialistic scientific worldview. As a microbiologist, his field of research does not, unlike that of modern physicists, transcend the normal boundaries of our patterns of thought; trust in the infallibility of human logic pervades Monod's brilliant work. (In exploring the weird domain of quantum physics, on the other hand, some physicists have begun to wonder whether, at its deepest levels, the universe really can be understood by human beings—or whether Haldane may not have been right all along, and things are indeed queerer than we can suppose.)

Monod's discoveries, which revealed the precise clockwork interaction of physical and chemical events within cells, have greatly enriched our understanding of living organisms. And his discoveries have convinced him that life itself has evolved through the interplay of chance and necessity alone. No internal vital forces and no external guiding principles exist. The forces at work are none other than those which govern inorganic chemical reactions.

Chance reigned supreme in the universe until random encounters of molecules created the first self-replicating macromolecule—DNA, deoxyribonucleic acid, the blueprint of life. From this point forward, the necessity of repeating the same combination (originally arrived at by chance), combined with the consequences of error in the replication process, began to diversify and enrich the universe in a new and systematic way. The evolution of life was and is something different from the nonliving processes that had occurred for billions of years before the first living things emerged, because it is directional. In the nonliving world, we see structures constructed and then dissolved, the cycle repeating itself over and over: tectonic forces thrust upward, creating mountains which are then eroded away over millions of years, after which the eroded material may once again be folded and forced upward, to begin the process of mountain building once more. Although the creation of complex elements from simple ones through the unimaginable heat within giant stars can be conceived as a directional process and is often included in the concept of evolution, that process comes to an end after only a few steps, with the radioactive disintegration of the heaviest elements that are created (uranium, thorium, and so forth). For billions of years, these elements are created and destroy themselves—endlessly, senselessly.

However, organic evolution—the evolution of living things—is truly directional in a completely new sense: no limits are set for the increase in complexity. Although cycles of life and death occur, constantly new and unexpected variations of organic construction continue to emerge. Most of these are not viable, but some of them turn out to be more successful than anything that existed before. This is the process of genetic variation and natural selection. Because simple organisms have already made use of all the opportunities open to them, survival chances of new forms of life depend in general upon their greater complexity. Evolving life is thus driven onward from simple to complex—naturally, automatically, without being directed through a higher mind or a higher plan.

Monod is careful to emphasize that true creation, or true emergence (the process described above), which occurs only through a first-time chance combination of genes, differs significantly from *epigenetic emergence,* which is encountered during the development of an organism. Epigenetic emergence occurs according to a plan. The genetic blueprint contained in the DNA of a successful survivor of chance creation instructs its descendants to develop the same form and internal organization. When these blueprints are altered through the impact of the radioactive particles that pervade the universe, or through the mixing effect of sexual reproduction, new elements of chance are injected into the evolutionary process. In the world of Monod, it is that endless interplay of chance and necessity, and nothing else, that thrusts evolution forward and leads to the continual emergence of new combinations and qualities, and to the incessant individualization of living organisms.

While epigenetic and true emergence might appear to have a superficial similarity, they are fundamentally different. Epigenetic emergence is guided not by chance but by chemical laws and affinities and is thus predictable and goal-directed. However, true emergence—the chance creation of various genes to begin with—is unpredictable. The probability of any particular gene being created is always practically zero before its combination, because an almost infinite number of possible chance combinations exist. Only *after* a gene has been created can its existence be explained through natural law. Monod therefore believes life may have arisen only once on earth and that once destroyed, it may never arise again. The odds against it are simply too great.

To be sure, other scientists argue that the emergence of life under conditions existing when the earth was young was almost inevitable. The odds against any one particular gene being created, they admit, were enormous; but, they add, any one of a large number of possible patterns would have been satisfactory, not just the particular combination that arose on the early earth. Some go so far as to maintain that the emergence of intelligence simply follows from competition among living organisms. But even if that is so, our position is still precarious; for if intelligence is a product of competition, then, according to the chemical physicist Aaron Kupperman, it becomes doubtful whether intelligent beings anywhere in the universe could have survived the dangerous stage of technological development currently reached by mankind without blasting themselves back into the Stone Age—or beyond.[3]

The very fact that intelligence *is* the product of ruthless competition makes it unlikely that anything but competition can be conceived of as desirable in the minds of intelligent beings, not only on earth but anywhere that life has arisen. "Intelligence is the most dangerous product of evolution," Kupperman argues, and he believes the unbreakable connection between intelligence and competition will seal the fate of our species—*unless* we concentrate all our efforts and use the limited time allotted to our species on earth to contact the different varieties of intelligence that may exist on other planets and learn their secrets. Alone, he believes, we are doomed. (These arguments reflect the traditional, materialistic worldview of science, stripped of all superfluous baggage and pursued to its logical conclusion.)

Thus, three alternative positions are possible: We might agree with Monod that true "creation"—the initial emergence of self-replicating molecules—is extremely rare and that life may have formed only once on earth. We might agree with other scientists who argue that life is common but the particular set of circumstances needed to produce intelligence is very rare. Or we might agree with Kupperman, who sees even the emergence of intelligence as a matter of course, but who sees intelligence infected, in its very evolution, with the germ of its own destruction.

No matter which position we take, the worldview of science seems uniquely suited to impress upon us the fragility of life on earth and hence to point to the necessity of safeguarding it. Here, however, we run up against the cardinal question to which materialistic science has no answer: *Why* should life be valued?

For Monod, meaning in a meaningless universe is provided through man's craving for objective knowledge, which must be elevated to become our highest ideal. Though it is "an anxious quest in a frozen universe of solitude," Monod demands that humanity summon the courage to follow this quest to its conclusion, rather than cling to prescientific myths and religions. Whenever science conflicts with traditional values and views of the world, those traditional values and worldviews must yield.

Even subjective experience is an illusion, which Monod would not eliminate (as long as it is recognized for what it is), because it is too much ingrained in our literature and our entire conception of reality. Other, more radical, materialists, especially the behaviorists, are less tolerant. In any case, the existence of consciousness—of subjective experience, of values—is ignored by those holding the worldview of traditional science.

Common sense revolts. To ignore consciousness—to dismiss subjective experience as a mirage—is to ignore the most important factor to emerge during life's long evolution.

The fact that there is no place in the traditional worldview of science for human consciousness does not mean, of course, that reductionists are amoral creatures oblivious to human values. They may be as principled as everyone else (or more so), but their values, if they have them, have been acquired without reference to their scientific views and are rarely acknowledged; there is nothing in their mind-brain philosophy to explain *why* they hold those values or why values are important. Textbooks ignore the issue; it is an irrelevancy, something which has no proper place in the "real world" as revealed by science. Life seems to go along smoothly enough without such values—or at least it did until we ran into the nuclear predicament.

But *why* do we care? *Why* do we value life so much? Is Monod's "anxious quest in a frozen universe of solitude"—the quest for objective knowledge—*all* that makes life worthwhile?

Relentless, intense pursuit of objective knowledge has led to one of the most profound discoveries: the human nervous system is limited; reality itself is vastly larger, far richer, and more varied than the small sector of it that our brain is able to perceive and comprehend.

Werner Heisenberg, who discovered the *uncertainty principle,* described the dawning of this insight in his book *Physics and Beyond.*[4] Here we meet scientists driven by a passionate desire to reveal the secrets of the final truth; they come closer and closer to their goal through superhuman effort, urged on by expectations which rise further at every step, and then—at the moment of highest suspense—encounter their own impotence in the face of the Ultimate.

The philosopher-economist Friedrich A. Hayek describes the matter more prosaically. While we know that a large variety of electromagnetic radiation of different wavelengths is emitted by different objects in the universe, our eyes can perceive and translate into conscious experience only a small fraction of those wavelengths, the visible spectrum. Likewise, our ears can pick up and translate into conscious experience only a very small fraction of the compression waves transmitted through the atmosphere. Some "sounds" are too deep for us to hear; some are of too high a frequency—too shrill. And only a minute part of all microscopic particles trigger our senses of taste and smell. From these inputs, and from information provided through the sense of touch, our brains construct their version of "reality." For survival within our environmental niche, we did not need anything more. Shaped by natural selection, the human brain is constructed to take note of only those stimuli from the environment that have bearing on the individual's survival, or, more precisely, those stimuli that contributed to the survival of human beings in the past and that are therefore perceived by their descendants' sense receptors. We cannot even imagine, suggests Hayek, what view of reality animals possessing receptors sensitive to different combinations of wavelengths or different types of microscopic particles might have; but their reality, too, would be only a small fraction of Reality itself, the fraction selected by the survival needs of the organism in question.[5]

The quest for Reality itself, therefore, recedes as a realistic objective for science; the quest for knowledge of matters essential to life's survival grows in importance. That new objective for science lifts one phenomenon to the very summit, a phenomenon which finds no place in traditional empirical science at all—the subjective experience of meaning; in a word, values.

The Worldview of Religion

I have a view of God as being infinitely merciful and kind. . . . My Christian hope is that God will hold off the dire results of our foolishness, pride, and stupidity; that provided that we humans convert, pray, and live decently (there will always be some good persons), the good Lord will spare us nuclear and other destructions. Briefly, I think God's goodness, love, and mercy will convert even the brightest of the hardheaded.
— Response of a Canadian professor of Religion, when asked about the values necessary for human survival.

Religion is a term encompassing a vast variety of perspectives. Not all, and perhaps not even most, of them are hostile to science, we are quick to point out. Nonetheless, it is true that in the most scientifically advanced societies—that is, the West— religions antagonistic to science have become very strongly established indeed. It is in the West that the world is most sharply divided; and, because of these societies' technological preeminence, it is their fate that will determine whether the species lives or dies. Thus we must narrow in on where the most threatening, most critical clash between worldviews has occurred.

Of course, there are religions that have a far wider focus than the views we will describe. To do justice to the worldview of religion in general, we would have to include Eastern religions. In these faiths, a personal God is generally absent. To be fair, that is also characteristic of the private convictions of nominal adherents to many creeds; and more modern, liberal versions of Christianity (such as process theology) tend to relegate a personal God to the background. Adherents to all these faiths, it might seem, are ready to meet the challenge of science halfway, so to speak, taking something of value from it and giving something in return. Many adherents to more traditional Western faiths are far less open, seeing science not as a challenge to widen intellectual horizons but as a threat to the foundation of faith itself.

Alarmed by the increasing emptiness and meaninglessness of

> Quote from the Need for a Sacred Science
> p. 72

human life brought about by the forward march of materialistic science, many such religious leaders have tried to reinstate or reinforce a belief in dualism—the idea that there are two separate worlds, one of matter and the other of mind or spirit. Under this dualistic conception of the world, the human soul is something that exists apart from the body and is usually thought to live on after the body's death. The concept of a spiritual realm directed by an omniscient and beneficent superhuman being—God—provides security and comfort to those able to believe in it. Therefore, it forms the basis of not only many older philosophies but also some more recent ones, and it has lately, through Nobel laureate and neuroscientist Sir John Eccles, even been brought into the world of science itself.

Eccles's ideas will be the first of three different religious worldviews we will discuss. Each view is progressively more extreme, more popular, and less compatible with science; all of them share, however, the traditional conception of God as an external being—in which way they differ from more liberal religions and philosophies.

Eccles, deeply troubled by the fate of humanity, is convinced that "mankind is sick and has lost faith in itself and in the meaning of existence."[6] A devout Catholic who dedicated his life to neuroscience after a profound religious experience at age eighteen, he suggested in 1977 a mind-brain theory based on holistic concepts—concepts to which Roger Sperry had introduced him in 1965. This came after decades of immersion— albeit for him disappointing immersion—in standard reductionistic research.

According to Eccles, parts of the brain's dominant, left hemisphere act like two-way radio sets. These parts contain *columns,* or *modules,* which can communicate with the self-conscious mind, though that communication is not continual; sometimes the link is open, sometimes it is closed. The mind exists separately and independently of brain activity. For Eccles, mind-brain separation has remained an axiomatic truth, a conviction unshaken by a lifetime of work in neuroscience.

Although Eccles concedes that the neocortex must reach a certain size and complexity for reflective thought to occur, he thinks that Darwinian evolutionary theory does not tell the whole story. The emergence of consciousness, he believes, is a "skeleton in the closet of orthodox evolution." A "divine providence" is actually at work, "operating over and above the materialistic happenings in biological evolution."[7]

In Eccles's view, the acquisition of self-consciousness, or the soul, occurred about one hundred thousand years ago. From then on, man knew he would have to die; and we see evidence of this revelation in the discovery of ceremonial burial sites dating from that age. Having achieved an awareness of death and the capacity for reflective thought, mankind gained access to a fundamentally different world: "Something had happened, mysteriously, wonderfully, in the evolution of the human brain to give it these potentialities which . . . we still are shocked by." In short, Eccles believes that, at this watershed in human history, man achieved direct contact with supernatural powers.[8]

While Monod is disturbed by the unrelenting hold of unsubstantiated belief and superstition on human action, Eccles is troubled by the inability of materialists and reductionists like Monod to "even recognize the extraordinary problem [of] living organisms acquiring mental experiences of a nonmaterial kind that are in another world from the world of matter-energy."[9] Science's failing is its inability to provide a philosophy outlining how mind can affect matter.[10] Human beings, for Eccles, did not come to exist by chance in a universe devoid of design. Nor are humans merely animals of a particularly complex kind. Able to experience the divine, humans become part of it. Only the existence of a soul, linked to the body yet able to range beyond the limited consciousness of animals—indeed, unfettered by the nature of matter and energy themselves—is sufficient explanation for the experiences only human beings can share. For Eccles, therefore, the human soul is "a divine creation which God attaches to the growing foetus at some time between conception and birth."[11]

Eccles does not believe human nature can survive Monod's "anxious quest in a frozen universe of solitude"—the search for objective knowledge in a world without meaning. The search for meaning lies at the core of human existence, and, Eccles believes, even a wrong interpretation that lends meaning to human experience is better than no meaning at all.[12] In science, as in religion, the dedicated search for meaningful answers to the questions posed by human life is what matters; and, seen as such a search, science becomes for Eccles a magnificent cultural endeavor of almost religious dimensions, a way of comprehending "the wonder and mystery of our existence as experiencing selves."[13]

This attitude toward science distinguishes Eccles from the large majority of materialistic scientists, who, as we have seen, generally downgrade the importance of subjective experience, of values, of those things that are considered in the realm of the spirit.

In his book *The Human Psyche,* Eccles singles out some of the arguments put forward by sociobiologists as, in his eyes, especially repulsive. Sociobiology achieved widespread attention—virtually bursting upon the scientific scene—in 1975 with the publication of Edward Wilson's monumental *Sociobiology: The New Synthesis,*[14] which immediately raised a storm of controversy. Wilson, a specialist in insects, tried to compare the behavior of social insects with the social behavior of other animals, including human beings—disregarding the fact, critics argued, that the differences between individuals in our species are incomparably greater than in any other species, particularly insect species. The main thrust of the criticism, however, was directed against Wilson's contention that human behavior is determined by genes to a far greater extent than previously assumed. Combined with a rather low, perhaps even base, estimate of human nature, put forward not so much by Wilson himself as by several of his supporters, that contention seemed unacceptable, not only to the religious but to those working in practically the entire range of the behavioral sciences. In fact, calm, objective discussion of the subject was impossible for many years.[15]

In Eccles's view, the sociobiologists' belief that humans differ from animals only in degree, not kind, is what leads them to describe "soft" altruism—the sort that refrains from the supreme step of self-sacrifice—as ultimately selfish and based on the expectation of being paid back. The sociobiologists go on to argue that underlying these actions are such psychological devices as pretence and deceit, including self-deceit.

With a deep pain that most of us would readily share, Eccles refers to this view of altruism, and of human nature generally, as "cynicism of a particularly obnoxious kind." He writes: "Instead of being the most gracious of human values, altruism is tainted with lying, pretense and deceit so that it is a monstrous hypocrisy."[16]

The sociobiologists' attitude underlines our conclusion that materialism cannot possibly tell us *why* life should be valued or *why* the preservation of mankind should be supported. And yet, will a mankind enjoying the comfortable protection of a "divine Providence" recognize its own responsibility?

Eccles argues that man is free to either accept or reject belief in supernatural guidance and that such freedom implies a "co-responsibility" for man's future. In that respect, however, Eccles is not typical of other dualists. He accepts science as a great cultural achievement, although he rejects it as an exclusive worldview. In spite of the materialistic and reductionistic orientation of practically all his colleagues, he remains convinced that objective knowledge is but a "secondary derivative of subjective experience" and that traditional humanitarian and Christian values remain.

That Eccles should maintain such a position in spite of his outstanding scientific achievements must impress upon even the staunchest materialists how much mind matters—how profoundly human thought and behavior can be molded and guided by values.

In contrast to the views of both believers in materialistic determinism and believers in providential guidance, Eccles's arguments for freedom are based on his conviction that subjective experience is primary. Freedom exists because men and women experience themselves as free. Eccles's dedication to the notion of human coresponsibility stems from his recognition of humankind's freedom of choice. For some other dualists, the belief that a supernatural power determines human fate eliminates this sense of freedom and responsibility.

Before we describe two examples of this kind of belief, we should point out that we know and sincerely admire many religious persons who are deep thinkers with a wide perspective and that we hold a high regard for the capacity of religion to reach beyond short-term aims and objectives. We know that this capacity, if hinged to the most urgent goal at present—that of protecting our earth—can be enormously effective in bringing about a more desirable attitude, because religion affects what traditional, materialistic science cannot touch: human emotions.

Perhaps it is our regard for this great potential of religion that leaves us pained by the refusal of a number of highly influential religious leaders to consider changes in our human situation that demand new approaches to values. It would be irresponsible to underestimate the danger of such refusal. Concern for the future demands that we face that danger forthrightly; and that will be our task for the balance of this chapter.

First, we will turn to Germain Grisez, who insists in his book *The Way of the Lord Jesus,* the first volume of his monumental series *Christian Moral Principles,* that the Word of God, as it has been interpreted by the Roman Catholic Church, must be followed without regard for any possible consequences, because the final results of our actions are known to God, and to God alone. Grisez's project originated in the late 1970s as an effort to answer Vatican II's call for a comprehensive reinvigoration of moral theology. The series as a whole—a work being completed with the support of thirty bishops, the Knights of Columbus, and other important Roman Catholic organizations—

is scheduled to be finished before this century's end. Its chief purpose is that it be used as a theological text by seminarians as well as interested Catholics, both priests and laypeople.

Grisez looks askance at any Roman Catholic work on moral theory that "is vitiated by substantial compromises with secular humanism." He intends to move Catholic thinking away from such liberalism back to unquestioned obedience to Christ's teachings as interpreted by the Church. Indeed, the foreword to the first volume concludes with the statement that "I hope no error will be found contrary to faith. . . . Everything I write— everything I think—I submit gladly and wholeheartedly to the better judgment of the Catholic Church."[17]

Throughout his book, Grisez examines in depth the practical ramifications of submitting oneself without question to God's will. For instance, both abortion and birth control—which might result in abortion if applied during the initial period of cell division—are fundamental evils. And what of those who warn of plagues, starvation, and disaster if population increase is not halted? Such predictions are utterly unsupportable, for only God can truly foresee the results of human actions. Indeed, Grisez feels obliged to warn against "following one's conscience," unless that conscience is molded by early training in Roman Catholic principles. Anything less is not enough. "A merely general knowledge of what is right and wrong simply does not provide sufficient moral guidance."[18]

What if the situation is such that unless an abortion is performed both a mother *and* unborn child will die? Should we save the mother's life at the expense of the child? Grisez holds that allowing only the child to die, not both, would amount to a "choice of the lesser evil," which we must reject as "consequentialism." Again, only God can know the ultimate results of any human action.

But what of the alternative: the mother refusing an abortion and dying, with her child, as a result? Would not her voluntary acceptance of death be, in fact, suicide in God's view and hence a mortal sin? Grisez replies that, though choosing the lesser of two evils would be obviously wrong, we can decide on a course of action, keeping in view *only the good consequences of what we do,* while ignoring those consequences that can be anticipated but that are *distinct* of what we choose. Human beings are responsible for their actions in only a limited sense: they can only be expected to see so far.

But Grisez immediately retracts any forceful support for what might be considered humane and compassionate considerations in situations like the one outlined above.

> My analysis points to the permissibility of certain operations which classical moralists would have excluded. I do not think this position is in significant conflict with received Catholic teaching. However, if my theory and the Church's teaching should in a particular case lead to inconsistent conclusions, I would follow and urge others to follow the Church's teaching rather than my theory. If the Church's teaching is open to legitimate refinement in the details of its applications, the refinement must be completed by those who exercise teaching authority in the Church.[19]

A Catholic is bound to obey the laws of the Church through a commitment made at baptism. That such a "commitment" is usually made shortly after birth and long before any critical faculties arise seems irrelevant.

While Grisez addresses university students and must be prepared for sophisticated counterarguments, there are those who hold the masses in their thrall, swaying public opinion at will. These moralists veto all independent thought. Their motivation may be utterly commendable; but the ridigity of their approach impedes rather than furthers progress toward more humane conditions on earth. They see their responsibility as a "head-on confrontation with the false view that material or energy, shaped by chance, is the final reality."[20] Such is the view of our second example, Francis A. Schaeffer, an influential Christian proselytizer. He has become well known through the publication of more than twenty books with millions of copies in print. His works have been translated into more than two dozen languages. Often lecturing at universities, Schaeffer was involved in founding the L'Abri fellowship, a Swiss retreat with affiliates in the United Kingdom, the Netherlands, Sweden, and the United States.

Like Eccles, Schaeffer is acutely aware of the superficiality and meaninglessness that have accompanied scientific advance. Unlike Eccles, he has no esteem for science, and he fails to distinguish between the wonder of discovering the pattern of natural law underlying the workings of the world and the damaging cynicism derived from a misplaced sense of superiority stemming from such discovery. Like Grisez's, Schaeffer's morality is one of utmost rigidity, but unlike the professor of philosophy, the religious revivalist considers reason itself as one of the major targets of attack. All of Schaeffer's work proclaims the uncompromising truth of historic, biblical Christianity, and his *Christian Manifesto* rallies the population and its government to turn back the tide of moral decadence and to change the course of history—by returning to biblical truth. This manifesto, which vehemently rejects the theory of evolution and other tenets of modern science, goes so far as to proclaim a state illegal that defies the "absolute law of God." He recommends legal and political action—possibly through massive demonstrations of civil disobedience—against such states.[21]

The fury Schaeffer directs against science is matched only by Monod's angry denunciation of religion. As the scientist wrote in *Chance and Necessity*:

> Armed with all the powers, enjoying all the riches they owe to science, our societies are still trying to live by and teach systems of values already blasted at the root by science itself.[22]

Such are the voices of a world divided, a world in helpless, hopeless combat with itself.

Reflections

Our problems are grave. Nonetheless, they have been caused by man and can be solved by man. What prevents their solution are two mutually incomprehensible worldviews, one rejecting facts in favor of ideals, the other rejecting ideals for the sake of facts. Rare voices of insight and responsibility seem unable to penetrate either camp. No ceasefire seems imminent.

The scientific worldview, embodied brilliantly in Jacques Monod's *Chance and Necessity,* seems bare of humane sentiment. Values are nonexistent. The religious worldview, on the other hand, is replete with values and seems to capture the essence of humanity—at least when human warmth is permitted to illuminate its core insights. But it lacks scientific credibility; it tells us more about the world we would like to live in than the world we actually inhabit.

Nonetheless, its attraction is so compelling that it induces a lifelong neuroscientist and Nobelist, John Eccles, to combine neuroscience with dualism; it leads a philosopher like Germain Grisez to renounce responsible concern for our descendants' fate on the grounds that God alone holds responsibility for a future only he can see; it causes a Christian revivalist like Francis Schaeffer to call for civil disobedience unless governments consent to be guided by biblical truth.

In such a world, a world divided, nuclear bombs breed in profusion; millions starve while irreplaceable topsoil erodes; and hope dissolves in mutual incomprehension.

⟶ Conclusion

Part 2

THE QUEST

The novelty of the aspirations he [the statesman] is articulating require him to use language in odd ways. An example is stoic talk about a "universal city". As it stands, this is a simple contradiction, and must have seemed absurd to many literal-minded Romans—as absurd as Galileo's talk, later on, about fixed stars that moved. But in a society dominated by a particular background structure, so that only small-scale political organizations seemed natural, how was someone to talk about this faintly perceived notion of a single world-wide society? Because the idea was new, there was no language to communicate it.

—William T. Jones

Once science modifies its traditional materialist-behaviorist stance and begins to accept in theory and to encompass in principle within its causal domain the whole world of inner conscious, subjective experience (the world of the humanities), then the very nature of science itself is changed. The change is not in the basic methodology or procedures, of course, but in the scope and content of science and in its limitations, in its relation to the humanities and in its role as a cultural, intellectual, and moral force.

—Roger Sperry

Prelude:
The More Encompassing Vision

For I have learned
To look on nature, not as in the hour
Of thoughtless youth; but hearing oftentimes
The still sad music of humanity,
Nor harsh nor grating, though of ample power
To chasten and subdue.

And I have felt
A presence that disturbs me with the joy
Of elevated thoughts; a sense sublime
Of something far more deeply interfused,
Whose dwelling is the light of setting suns,
And the round ocean and the living air.
—William Wordsworth

Roger Sperry looks at human problems from a larger perspective, one that brings into focus not only all of mankind but all of life—and beyond that, all of creation. From this vantage point, he sees humanity as a small but extraordinary fragment of reality, endowed with the gift of mind—probably the most amazing product of evolution—but wasting that gift and, indeed, on the verge of destroying it. Sperry sees warring worldviews defending facts against ideals or ideals against facts as part of a larger whole, as incomplete fractions of the same reality. Such an encompassing vision, which sees mankind as embedded in the web of nature, created through its forces and itself creating through its forces, leads to a new realm of understanding. Reality is seen ruthlessly eliminating all unrealistic expectations (that is, expectations that fail to take account of nature's laws) while at the same time condemning to subhuman conditions those without *any* expectations, ideals, or values. In this new realm, ideals and facts must support each other; they cannot exist in mutual exclusion, except to the detriment of mankind.

In Sperry's view, "unrealistic expectations" are created not only by belief in supernatural powers, but also by unwarranted confidence in the ability of materialistic, reductionistic science to compensate for the loss of such beliefs. In all higher organisms, in all beings whose nervous systems are consciously involved in the making of choices, the laws of nature leave room for a conception of meaning and purpose. We need values, Sperry is convinced, to provide our lives with direction; and such values must be informed by science, to avoid waste, suffering, and degradation of life.

His vision of reality includes the insight that the forces of nature discovered by science are the same as those attributed to God by religion. However, instead of being led through that insight to share the hollow and destructive cynicism of so many scientists, Sperry feels a profound sense of awe and wonder. Through early adventures in the wilderness, he has become deeply attached to nature, and he finds in his reason, his knowledge, and his understanding reinforcement for that attachment rather than dilution of it.

> In the eyes of science, to put it simply, man's creator becomes the vast interwoven fabric of all evolving nature, a tremendously complex concept that includes all the immutable and emergent forces of cosmic causation that control everything from high-energy subnuclear particles to galaxies, not forgetting the causal properties that govern brain function and behavior at individual and social levels. For all these, science has gradually become our accepted authority, offering a cosmic scheme that renders most others simplistic in comparison and which grows and evolves as science advances.[1]

In his view of nature, Sperry merges aspects of traditional pantheism—that is, the equation of nature with God or Creation—with contributions of his own based mainly on his research and philosophical contemplation of the mind-brain relationship.

This is the view, in short, that may help bridge the gap between the world of science and that of religion; and it is the view we shall explore in detail throughout the rest of this book.

· 3 ·
The Lure of the
Mind-Brain Problem

All the ultimate aims and values of mankind could be profoundly affected by a thoroughgoing rational insight into the mind-body relationship. It was the broad significance of the problem as much as the difficulty of reaching a solution that prompted William James to declare that the attainment of a genuine glimpse into the mind-brain relation would constitute "the scientific achievement before which all past achievements would pale."   —Roger Sperry

The winner of the 1981 Nobel Prize for medicine and physiology began his career in the humanities. After graduating from Oberlin College in 1935 as a major in English literature, Roger Sperry switched to psychology for his master's studies, also at Oberlin. It was here that he first developed what was to become a lifelong interest in the enigma of mind and brain, sparked by a remarkable intellect, Raymond H. Stetson, chairman of the psychology department. For his doctoral work, Sperry switched to biology, attracted to the laboratory of the eminent Paul A. Weiss at the University of Chicago, who was then propounding a radically new theory about how the brain works. When Sperry completed his Ph.D., he moved to the laboratory of a prominent psychologist of the time, Karl S. Lashley, to do postdoctoral research work, first at Harvard and then for six years at the Yerkes Laboratory in Florida, a facility jointly administered by Harvard and Yale. During the Florida years he worked with such influential persons as the Canadian psychologist Donald O. Hebb.

Sperry next returned to the University of Chicago for six years as an assistant professor in anatomy, then worked under Seymour Kety as section chief in Neurological Diseases and Blindness at the National Institutes of Health, and finally, in 1954, accepted a position at the California Institute of Technology as first Hixon Professor of Psychobiology. The Hixon fund had been established in 1938 to promote the study of those aspects of biology dealing with human behavior.

Concern with the Brain

Sperry's pioneering work relevant to the development of the brain's neural pathways—the wiring of the brain, so to speak—and his later unfolding of new knowledge regarding the differences between the right and left hemispheres of the brain—his *split-brain* work—are known worldwide. Though not our primary focus, this earlier work deserves mention in passing to provide a sense of the background to the mind-brain theory.

Sperry first gained attention in the early forties, when he discovered that, contrary to prevailing opinion, nerves are not functionally interchangeable; their original connections are important. A nerve pathway can't simply be switched from one task to another; how it was originally wired defines its function.[1]

Next, he turned to the question of how these hard-wired connections get established in the first place. Was it through learning by trial and error before birth, as psychologists claimed; or was it inherited, as ethologists argued? This inquiry led to his second outstanding contribution to neuroscience, the *chemo-affinity theory* of how the brain's neural network develops. In short, those networks of nerve cells (or neurons) that direct behavior are wired into the brain under the precise chemical guidance of the genes. The genes—the basic hereditary mechanisms of all living things—are the electricians; the neural network is the circuit board.

In 1954 Sperry described his experiments and presented his

theory at an international biochemical symposium at Oxford.[2] The heated discussion that followed began with Seymour Kety declaring that "Dr. Sperry's work is always provocative, and this is no exception." Attacks prevailed. At one point, Ralph W. Gerard, recalling a violent argument with Paul Weiss about his resonance theory, after which the two scarcely spoke with one another for the remainder of his visit, noted that "the chemical interpretation in some ways is even more dramatic and revolutionary." Sperry's conclusion that billions and billions of individually labeled nerve cells would home in on preprogrammed goals seemed simply impossible.

Years later, however, after being thoroughly verified by hundreds of repeated tests, the theory entered the standard texts on the subject. Even now, after nearly fifty years have passed, appreciation of this work is still growing. In 1989, Sperry received the National Medal of Science from the President of the United States for "work on neurospecificity which showed how the intricate brain networks for behavior are effected through a system of chemical coding of individual cells, which has made fundamental contributions to the understanding of human nature."[3] Sperry himself tends to look back on this work as more radical and more basic than the later split-brain research.

Specialists in related areas have recreated the competitive atmosphere that prevailed in those formative years.[4] It was then, according to Robert Doty, one of Sperry's former students and a psychologist at the University of Rochester Medical Center's Center of Brain Research, that Sperry "invented the experimental paradigms that people have used for the last thirty years."[5] Sperry's doctoral mentor, Paul Weiss, was claiming that his experiments demonstrated that the brain functions independently of specific nerve connections. To explain this, he proposed the "resonance principle," by which neurons become attuned to respond in a way analogous to the broadcasting and reception of radio waves. Had it been true, Weiss's resonance theory would have replaced the prevailing switchboard-connection theories of how neurons function. All textbooks would have had to be rewritten. That did not happen. Instead, Sperry's immersion in the problem led to a rival theory which became, in colleague Viktor Hamburger's words, "one of the few important general unifying principles in today's developmental neurobiology."[6]

But it was not only Weiss whose ideas would be successfully challenged by Sperry, then a twenty-five-year-old doctoral candidate. Karl Lashley's theory of *cortical equipotentiality*, which held that each part of the cortex is equally well suited to take over any task, met the same fate. Hamburger, in awarding the Ralph Gerard Prize of the National Society for Neuroscience to Sperry, pointed out, "I know of nobody else who has disposed of cherished ideas of both his doctoral and his post-doctoral sponsor, both at that time the acknowledged leaders in their fields."[7]

Sperry, however, did not rest on these triumphs. His colleagues in microbiology thought he should try to find the molecular basis of chemoaffinity, the theory that developing neurons are guided to their targets through individual chemical attraction. But Sperry resisted the prevalent tendency in science "to find out more and more about less and less." His policy was to keep the big questions in mind by asking continuously, "What difference does it make?—especially ten, twenty, or more years from now?"[8] He pointedly shunned crowded competitive fields where he felt the goals were neatly laid out and success inevitable, the only remaining question being who might happen to get there first. He preferred the challenge—and the loneliness—of asking new questions and being the first in a new area.

Therefore, when success finally rewarded him—when his theory had become the leading one in developmental biology, when it was being transmitted through all the textbooks on the subject to thousands of students in every country on earth, when Monod in *Chance and Necessity* was referring to Sperry's efforts as "remarkable experimental work," when tests in hundreds of laboratories were being based on his pioneering efforts—Sperry himself had already moved on to a new field in neuroscience, one in which his impact would become even greater.

This was his split-brain research. It involved the surgical splitting of the brain by cutting the corpus callosum, the "bridge" connecting the left and right hemispheres. This largest bundle of fibers in the brain contains some two hundred million nerve fibers, but until the 1950s its function had defied every explanation. Reports that completely severing it in human patients caused no detectable symptoms, even with extensive testing, had turned it into the enigma of the decade in mind-brain science and had led to theories of the wildest sort.

Of course, the puzzle attracted Sperry and his students, and with meticulous new surgical and testing procedures they managed to reverse previous conclusions, leading to unforeseen and dramatic results. As they explored the consequences of severing the corpus callosum in monkeys and cats, they were able to show that each half of the brain perceives, learns, and remembers separately, as if two conscious minds exist within one cranium. Split-brain animals (and later persons) could even perform mutually contradictory mental tasks at the same time.[9]

Human subjects became available for testing in the 1960s after neurosurgeons Philip Vogel and Joseph Bogen in Los Angeles performed operations called *commissurotomies* to relieve intractable epileptic seizures. Exhaustive studies of the intricate higher faculties in man as they relate to each hemisphere could now be performed, with quite unexpected results: while dominance in speech, writing, and calculation in the left hemisphere was expected, the discovery of the right hemisphere's superiority in many important aspects of thought, such as visual-spatial tasks, music, and so forth, came as a major surprise. The distinctively different approach of each hemisphere toward a task was striking. The left hemisphere of the brain was found to be the seat of "analytic step-by-step reasoning" while a more synthetic, "all-at-once-grasp of a situation" was a product of the right hemisphere. This interpretation spread like wildfire, with the American Psychological Association calling Sperry's work "epochal" in presenting him with its Distinguished Scientific Contribution Award.

Perhaps the most fascinating conjecture arising from the intensive study of these newly discovered right-hemisphere faculties was that the mute half of the brain plays a dominant role in forming the basis of aesthetic, emotional, and even religious perspectives—underlying processes inaccessible to logical analysis and yet fundamental to human interrelationships, and probably central to today's global predicament.

Not only the scientific community (where reports about split-brain research from as far away as Japan could soon be found in the *Psychological Abstracts*) became excited, but also the general population, which adopted the right hemisphere as a symbol for freedom from what many perceived and decried as the "oppression" of analytical thought. Books and papers on the topic were published in abundance.[10] Being solid and repeatable, Sperry's discoveries on hemispheric differences entered the textbooks quickly, just as his discoveries in brain development had before; but this time they were accompanied by a widespread fascination with the subject matter throughout much of society.[11]

Eminent scientists as well as the general public agreed on the importance of Sperry's work. Monod, who had already been attracted to Sperry's studies of neural regeneration, referred to his split-brain work, too, with the greatest respect and was able, in spite of his strongly reductionist attitudes, to fully recognize its implications. He drew special attention to the discovery that in "difficult tests that involve matching the three-dimensional shape of an object held in either hand to . . . a two-dimensional picture of that object projected onto a screen, the aphasic right hemisphere proved itself far superior to the 'dominant' left hemisphere—not just more accurate, but able to discriminate more rapidly." Monod maintains that "it is tempting to speculate upon the possibility that the right hemisphere is responsible for an important part, perhaps the more 'profound' part, of subjective simulation."[12]

From the opposite philosophical camp, John Eccles joined Monod, referring to Sperry's split-brain work as "the most remarkable investigations ever made on human brains."[13] A new perspective on the threshold between science and philosophy had been gained.

Not without good reason, therefore, did the Nobel Committee in Sweden select Sperry for its prestigious prize, stating, "His work has provided us with an insight into the inner world of the brain which hitherto has almost been hidden from us."[14]

Yet still more important were the implications of Sperry's discoveries for the unexplored potentials of the human mind.

·4·
Concern with Consciousness

Our knowledge is an island in the infinite ocean of the unknown.
— Victor Weisskopf

The Larger Perspective

At the height of his success, Sperry reacted in a fashion intensely typical of his character: he stepped forward beyond all his previous work to accept the challenge of a far greater, more difficult, and more important task. He even went so far as to call all his previous efforts "relatively minor in their implications" compared to his present concern with consciousness, ethics, and values.[1]

His thoughts on the matter, and the conclusions he reached, led him not only to turn over to eager investigators a second field in neuroscience, which he had opened through his pioneer experiments, but also compelled him to reach beyond the comparatively secure field of verifiable science itself and enter a new domain: philosophy. It was in the late fifties and early sixties that Sperry first expressed thoughts previously unheard-of in his field—thoughts that would later take over his undivided interest and that would eventually reverberate in the minds of many serious thinkers. When Sperry conceived these thoughts, however, he was far ahead of his time, in unfamiliar territory, struggling, alone with no support but what he had learned through his lifelong concern with mind and brain and the indomitable conviction that what he thought and said was true and important. But now he was not only fighting against restrictive, claustrophobic, clashing worldviews; he was also battling against a slowly progressive paralysis, primary lateral sclerosis, a disease about which he knew every detail through his professional training—most of all that it was incurable.

Suffering was not unknown to Sperry; nor was this the first time he had cured himself—or at least forced the symptoms of his disease from his awareness—through unconventional means. In 1950, before he was forty years old, diagnosis of tuberculosis forced him to check in to the Trudeau Sanatorium in Upper New York State, where he did not resign himself to the conventional bed-rest regimen. Instead, with the permission of the institution's director, he treated himself with a mixture of mental effort and outdoor activity. During this year he wrote his first paper on consciousness, a theme that already pervaded his interests.

> At the core of all metaphysical problems stands the mind-brain relationship, real understanding of which could have vast influences on all the ultimate aims and values of mankind.[2]

The treatise itself, "Neurology and the Mind-Brain Problem," refuted a theory called *psychoneural isomorphism* and replaced it with a functionalist theory, which anticipated what today has become the leading view in philosophy.[3] Psychoneural isomorphism is the view that brain patterns are something like miniature copies of perceived or imagined objects, and that the conscious meaning we attach to objects derives from this correspondence. The view described by Sperry, in contrast, sees consciousness as a product of the very way in which the brain functions, as its "interaction with the object," as a means developed by the brain to handle incoming information about the outside world.[4]

This early paper aroused attention, yet it did not shock. The reaction to his later more daring, more encompassing, more controversial conclusions, however, was different.

Having pronounced his new view for the first time during a conference discussion in 1958,[5] Sperry began affirming it—at first cautiously in 1964, then more boldly from 1965 onward. Every one of his papers on consciousness emphasizes two key postulates.

1. The mind, or consciousness, as an emergent property of brain function, interacts *causally* at its own mental level. In other words, mind emerges from matter, but mind interacts in mental terms—in terms of thought and ideas, not neural activities.

2. Consciousness exerts downward control over brain activity in an encompassing, supervenient sense. In short, mind controls matter.

Or, expressed with utmost simplicity:

Mind emerges from matter.

Thoughts and ideas interact at their own level.

Mind controls matter.

With these few simple postulates, a new worldview was born, intermediate between materialism and dualism: practical, fruitful, common-sense oriented, and closer to objectively described *and* subjectively perceived reality than anything previously expressed. In the years that followed, Sperry clarified his views, discussed and debated them, and explored their far-reaching implications—including their effects on the kinds of values we live for and govern by.

Value Implications

Our world faces immense problems as it enters the twenty-first century. What would be the response, Sperry questions, if we could call upon the services of an "extraterrestrial trouble-shooter," free of our human foibles and prejudices? Such a being, he believes, would quickly narrow in on one crucial factor: the values that motivate and justify our actions.

> The trends toward disaster in today's world stem mainly from the fact that while man has been acquiring new, almost godlike powers of control over nature, he has continued to wield these same powers with a relatively shortsighted, most ungodlike set of values, rooted, on the one hand, in outdated biologic hangovers from evolution in the Stone Age, and, on the other hand, in various mythologies and ideologies.[6]

What remedy would the alien suggest? That we adjust the values we hold so that they are more compatible with current views of how the world works and more useful in helping us solve the terrible problems that confront us.

Like the alien he imagines, Sperry looks at human problems independently, distancing himself as far as possible from all commonly accepted assumptions, prejudgments, and prejudices. He applies to values the same mental attitude that led to his breakthroughs in science. In fact, he goes farther. He does not separate science from values at all, believing that the creative forces of nature may arouse the same sort of awe that has since ancient times been reserved for supernatural powers.

In addition, his philosophical contemplations, initially focused on the mind-brain relationship, discover more general truths as their focus widens.

As we have seen, the concepts of *emergence* and of *downward causation* are central to the understanding of Sperry's philosophy. These describe something generally overlooked by reductionistic scientists: the appearance of new laws and properties at every level of organization in nature and the interaction of these laws and properties with all those that had previously evolved.

Instead of a succession of linear cause-effect relationships from particles to brain activity to behavior (with no place for consciousness, values, or meaning), the new worldview takes into account that a complex system of mutual interrelationships exists, in which each new creation becomes a new determining factor. It leads us into a world far more realistic than that of either materialism or dualism.

While the concept of emergence dispenses with any need for external, supernatural powers to account for the phenomenon of creation, it simultaneously demands more respect for the reality and autonomous vigor of new entities than traditional science has allowed. In other words: emergents are not inert; they *act*. They are involved in a constant reshifting of events in our universe. The world of *emergent causation* is the dynamic, living, real world. This is the world in which the emergence of life changed the atmosphere, increased the ratio of oxygen to nitrogen, and led to the extinction of nitrogen-dependent organisms and the rise of oxygen breathers. This is the world in which the emergence of consciousness changed the relationship of man with nature and of man with man. This is the world in which the freedom of choice we experience becomes an active factor in evolution.

The Concept of Emergence

A thorough grasp of the concepts of emergence and of downward causation is crucial if we are to understand what Sperry is driving at.

The *Random House Dictionary* defines *emergence* as "the appearance of new properties in the course of development or evolution that could not have been foreseen at an earlier stage." One example of the process is the appearance of liquidity in water through the combination of hydrogen and oxygen. Water is wet—and "wetness" is an emergent property.

Some critics object that wetness does not exist unless created through the interaction of water molecules with our sense of touch. Nor do taste, sound, light, or colors exist unless taste receptors, ears, or eyes are involved. Therefore, they argue, the entire concept of emergence is questionable. That objection, however, is invalid. Water, undeniably, is able to cause a feeling of wetness when in contact with organs of touch—a property hydrogen or oxygen in isolation do not possess. Taste, sound, light, and colors emerge through the interaction of natural elements with other sense organs. That sense organs are needed to bring them about is no argument against the emergence of these sensations as such.

Whether or not our sense organs are affected by newly emergent properties and characteristics does not change the fact that these properties and characteristics affect one another. With each chance creation of new phenomena through first-time constellations of atoms and molecules, with each new combination of interactions among their forces, new determining factors come into play. For instance, the characteristic of "liquidity" is an emergent property of water that is not dependent on the senses (as opposed to "wetness"). Because of this property of liquidity, water is able to dissolve sodium chloride and form an electrolytic conductor. Neither hydrogen nor oxygen alone is able to do this, yet this has nothing to do with the effect of either on the sense organs.

The concept of emergence itself is not new. The *Encyclopaedia Britannica* (fifteenth edition) attributes the first notion of this natural principle to John Stuart Mill, who favored it over *associationism,* the then-dominant view of reality. Under this view, nearly everything we are familiar with is a combination of simpler entities. These components each include a vital aspect, or part, of the new whole. Mill, on the other hand, held that in forming the new whole, the individual parts may well be stripped of their identities, while at the same time the character of the whole object emerges. Wilhelm Wundt termed Mill's notion *creative synthesis;* later yet, it was labeled *emergence.*

The philosopher of science George Henry Lewes differentiated *emergents,* whose final nature could not be predicted from their parts, from *resultants*—combinations like sand and talcum powder—whose properties could be forecast. At that time, in the mid-1800s, the characteristics of chemical compounds were thought to be impossible to predict from the nature of their constituents. For instance, salt is not in the least like either chlorine or sodium. But this conclusion was undermined as new and more sophisticated models of the atom were devised. Such models, based on quantum theory, could predict the characteristics of chemical compounds. Therefore, philosophers now distinguish between two kinds of emergence: a *weak* form which can be reconciled with materialism, and a *strong* form which cannot.[7] Much of the misunderstanding and criticism of Sperry's position—discussed in detail in later chapters—finds root in this controversy surrounding the concept of emergence.

Around 1900, the concept was used by the French philosopher Henri Bergson, among others, and ascribed to as yet unknown powers working in the universe, such as the *élan vital*, a force thought to be connected with living things and distinct from the well-known natural forces studied by physics. Once tainted with mysticism, the entire idea of emergence was rejected by the scientific community, together with everything supernatural or even abstract. Worldviews such as materialism, positivism, and behaviorism, with their extreme concentration on tangible things and their disregard and ridicule of ideals, of values—even of consciousness itself—became dominant. So influential was the unreserved admiration of traditional science's soaring successes in the inorganic and lower organic world, that these views were able to hold the behavioral sciences in their thrall for fifty years, even though they were increasingly perceived as unsatisfactory and the concept of emergence had long since been liberated from its mystical and dualistic connotations.[8]

Sperry's conception of emergence and emergent evolution is fully compatible with modern science. At the same time, he feels that an event or phenomenon can mean something only if the overall guidance of its parts is understood and perceived as emanating from a higher level. If we speak and think about our actions as determined by the physicochemical interplay of atoms and molecules within our brains and bodies, reality remains senseless and nothing will be achieved. Nothing is even worth achieving. But if we speak and think about them in terms of values and ideals, these same events acquire an enormous power and potency—although the laws of nature remain in effect.

Thoughts and Ideas

Scientists find it difficult to accept the postulate that thoughts and ideas created by the mind—once it has emerged from brain activity—interact with one another at their own level. Is Sperry really thinking of the mind in a dualistic sense after all: disembodied, divorced from the physical brain, an inhabitant of a world apart?

Quite the contrary. Sperry has repeatedly emphasized that the mind is invariably tied to, and a part of, the living brain. Thus, while thoughts and ideas in the mind interact at their own level, physical and chemical changes in the brain occur simultaneously. The crucial difference between Sperry and materialistic neuroscientists is that he sees mental interaction as a newly emerged phenomenon of primary importance, with chemical changes being secondary; while materialists argue that events occur the other way around, with physical and chemical changes of first importance and mental action a superfluous byproduct.

In Sperry's view, decisions produced through conscious effort guide the organization of brain activity in a way that would be impossible without such effort. All cultural achievements are results of conscious thought and could not have occurred without it.

That does not make Sperry's position a dualistic one. He retains a one-world view in which each newly emergent phenomenon is causally active—from atoms formed from nuclear particles to the most profound ideals created by the functioning of the brain at a level beyond which our physical investigations can reach: the level of the mind.

The Concept of Downward Causation

Sperry himself considers the concept of *downward causation* his own most significant contribution to the understanding of the mind-brain relationship and to the philosophy of ethics.

Downward causation describes how the properties of the whole determine the fate of its parts—parts whose organization created the whole to begin with. The relationship is always a two-way street: mutual, reciprocal, and simultaneous. That is, downward causation does not *supplant* the laws and properties associated with single parts; instead, it provides a new and more dominant *organizing principle.* As Sperry sees it, *mental properties*—thoughts, values, and so forth—do not interfere in the functioning of individual brain cells. Rather, they *supervene.*[9] To supervene means to give overall direction to physical processes without disturbing them, in much the same way that a computer program directs the machine's output or a television program controls the patterns of light and dark formed on the screen (examples used by Sperry in several of his papers).

Using more current philosophical terms, Sperry has spoken of *micro-properties* (properties of the parts) being overridden by *macro-properties* (properties of the whole).

> What matters is that the movement and fate of the parts . . . once the whole is formed, are thereafter governed by entirely new macro-properties and laws that previously *did not exist,* because they are properties of a new configuration.[10]

For instance, consider the situation of living cells carried through the air in the wing of an eagle. The cells alone would not be able to fly; their organization into the wing of a bird makes that feat possible. The properties of the new whole, the bird and its wing, determine the fate of the cells that created it. Or consider a forest. The size and shape of each tree is determined by the proximity of other trees around it. The accumulation of humus in the ground depends upon trees providing enough protection from the wind to keep leaves from blowing away. The moisture content, amount of shade or sunshine, and the flora and fauna within a forest are all determined by properties of the forest as a whole, while at the same time each of these particulars, as it affects the others, becomes a cocreator of this one entity: the forest. It is this wonderful, near-mystical interweaving of causes and effects, in which being, becoming, and creating are one, that underlies the phenomena of emergence and downward causation.

Sperry's favorite example is that of a wheel rolling downhill and carrying its atoms and molecules along, "whether they like it or not."[11] Since that example can be explained through the exact knowledge of single-part properties—those of the wheel, the hill, the earth's gravity, and so on—it has often been rejected as too simplistic and as making the concept of downward causation superfluous. Downward causation acquires its full significance only where the complexity of the situation and the accumulation of unknowns make all other explanations crude distortions of reality.

Emergent Causation

Put emergence and downward causation together and you have the core of a new and different worldview—*emergent causation*. The term has, as far as we know, not previously been used as a label for Sperry's philosophy as a whole,[12] but we feel it is a good overall description of Sperry's new unifying vision of reality. For one thing, it is handy to have a simple, short expression to differentiate Sperry's viewpoint from other positions, such as materialism, dualism, and so forth. And, too, the phrase is equally applicable to his mind-brain theory and to his philosophy of ethics.

Action and Reaction

The test of a scientific theory is its ability to withstand debate—to emerge, stronger and purer, from what some have called the crucible of ideas. Certainly Newton's observation that every action gives rise to an equal and opposite reaction seems to hold in the realm of ideas as well as in that of physics.

Not surprisingly, then, Sperry's ideas of emergent causation caused immediate controversy in the scientific community. Indeed, the first reaction among Sperry's colleagues was one of nearly universal rejection, particularly of his contention that consciousness causally affects brain activity. One of Sperry's former graduate students from the 1960s related how disturbed his coworkers had been when Sperry advanced his views. The group of them, fearing their own reputations—and career prospects—would suffer together with that of their superior, joined in excited discussions on how to dissuade him from expressing his views in public. Yet, while they debated, he had already crossed that bridge.

In 1964, at a lecture at the American Museum of Natural History in New York entitled "Problems Outstanding in the Evolution of Brain Function," the audience was astonished to hear a neuroscientist as distinguished as Roger Sperry express the view that, although no interference with natural laws is involved, the human brain's powers of perception, cognition, reason, judgment, and the like have to be accepted, *even in the world of science,* as dominating and directing the forces operating among individual atoms, molecules, and cells.[13]

In fact, Sperry had first publicly expressed his views on consciousness as early as 1958, during a conference on the central nervous system and behavior. Here, Sperry stated that he had always been dissatisfied with the prevalent assumption in the behavioral sciences that conscious subjective experience could be disregarded when describing brain functioning. He defended his conviction that to have any effect, a stimulus has to be sensed and felt subjectively: "In other words the animal must feel the pain from the shock, must smell or taste the meat juice, and so on." Such "subjective awareness" is a product of the long evolution of the nervous system, and it exists—and persists—"because it does serve a real use." Subjective experience helps us to act more effectively in the world.[14] Although Sperry defended his new understanding of consciousness as causal during this conference, which was dominated by staunch stimulus-response behaviorists, the atmosphere at that time was too hostile for immediate impact. If any member of the symposium was moved by Sperry's convictions, the reflection occurred in silence.

Why was this? In the late 1950s and early 1960s, behaviorism, materialism, and reductionism ruled supreme in the behavioral sciences. Consciousness was dismissed as irrelevant if not nonexistent. "The nature of subjective experience" was a "minor problem soon to vanish," declared B. F. Skinner in 1963. "The mentalism that survives in the form of sensation and perception will disappear as alternative techniques are proved valuable in analyzing stimulus control," he argued, on the grounds that if "the evidence of consciousness and reasoning could be explained in other ways in animals, why not also in man?"[15] A defender of logical positivism, Dean E. Wooldridge, wrote that "it is not clear that the behavior of any individual or the course of world history would have been affected in any way if awareness were non-existent." Although nature has, "in the last million years or so, been able to afford *homo sapiens* the luxury of employing the small portion of his nervous equipment that can be spared from really essential duties for pursuing the hobby that we have named the 'higher mental activities,' " Wooldridge concluded that "no useful purpose has yet been established for the sense of awareness."[16] And "living organisms, including human beings, are simply very complicated physico-chemical mechanisms," added John Smart, the latter-day defender of La Mettrie's motto: Man Is a Machine.[17]

Not a trace of understanding for the importance and influence of emergent properties is found in any of these views. And these declarations were not those of isolated persons; they represent a viewpoint that dominated higher education and with it the entire worldview of the West.

The psychologist Sigmund Koch complained—still in 1964—

that classical behaviorism had phrased "every mentalist category distinguished in the history of thought, including, I think, the medieval scholars," in stimulus-response terms; that these tendencies did not diminish, but flourished, under neobehaviorism; and that "neo-neo-behaviorism" was "now upon us," and the situation was growing worse.[18] As a result, he feared, psychology was becoming "an object of derision" and a "mass-dehumanization process."[19]

Any efforts to counter this situation were either not widely enough known or so unscientific and incredible that they were met with only scorn and ridicule. The worries of members of Sperry's group were therefore well founded, as they buried themselves eagerly in the unearthing of new information. The harder they worked, however, and the more they found, the more Sperry saw his assumptions supported. Not only did the right hemisphere seem to display a new form of thinking, a vivid grasp of essentials not matched by the "superior" left, but *both* sides of the brain were capable of creating complete images from the scantiest input.[20] "Awareness" thus seemed to be far more than simply a stimulus-evoked reaction; it seemed to involve a definite element of creation.

From a more distant and uninvolved position, Viktor Hamburger expressed his own assessment of the situation with insight and humor.

> Roger Sperry himself in his intrepid way, fearing neither gods nor philosophers, has worked out an entire novel *theory of consciousness*—which is scientifically acceptable and avoids the pitfalls of psycho-physical parallelism and reductionist materialism. It confers on the conscious mind a *causal* role in regulating brain processes. This puts scientific determinism in an entire new light and will lead necessarily to a reassessment of the problem of high philosophical priorities such as free will, value judgments, in short, the *humanistic* aspects of human nature.[21]

Long before Sperry expressed his controversial views on consciousness openly, long before his split-brain research had re-

moved his last doubt and hesitation, he had harbored his assumptions internally. Although the word itself was not yet
used, the concept of *emergence* was already implicit in Sperry's
1952 paper "Neurology and the Mind-Body Problem," where
consciousness was explained as a product of the active, functioning, living brain, ready to respond to the outside world. The
idea itself is very close to the concept of consciousness as causal,
consciousness as necessary for the decision-making process.

The idea of consciousness as causal was expressed more dis-
tinctly in Sperry's 1964 James Arthur Lecture on the evolution
of the human brain, at the American Museum of Natural History in New York, and again during a study week entitled
"Brain and Conscious Experience" at the Vatican in Rome,
where it occurred for the first time in connection with the term
emergence.[22]

The concept was made explicit and presented in the form of
a mind-brain theory for the first time in 1965[23] and was by then
already linked to Sperry's rejection of the science-values dichotomy.

Sperry's new views had been brought about through years of
wrestling with the problem, through meditative immersion in
the results of his split-brain research, through habits of independent thinking, and through a common-sense approach that
refused to accept any distortion of reality to accommodate it to
prevailing theory.

Such habits of mind are essential prerequisites to any fundamental change in worldviews—or, as the philosopher of science Thomas Kuhn puts it, any shift of paradigm. In his *Structure of Scientific Revolutions,* Kuhn explains that "after a paradigm
is conceived, nature is forced into it" and only "if the paradigm
fails, the vision is widened."[24] Kuhn also argues that new theories are generally preceded by one or two decades of crisis.[25]

In the mid-sixties, more than two decades of crisis had indeed passed since the idea of the mind as causal, so self-evident
to all religions and to all humanist philosophies previously, had
given way to that of the nonexistence of the mind (or at least

the nonpotency of it) in the worldview of the materialists, logical positivists, and most of all the behaviorists. A return to the past was impossible. Because science was demonstrably more fruitful in the search for truth—because it produced results—it had replaced religion as the West's major belief system, at least among the intellectual elite. Yet, science seemed to have little productive to say when applied to interhuman relations. The influential reign of stimulus-response behaviorism was perceived as particularly degrading to traditional ideas of human dignity and decency.

For many, clinging to two separate and mutually contradicting views of the world remained the only alternative; yet such attempts merely led one deeper into an impossible situation rather than resolving it. While C. P. Snow's well-known and influential book *The Two Cultures and the Scientific Revolution* vividly portrayed the disastrous effect on our society of the split between science and the humanities,[26] the philosopher William T. Jones drew attention to the possibility of even greater difficulties if that conflict were to fight itself out *within* the conscience of a single individual. He saw the internalized tension between scientific and humanistic conceptions of reality as a source of "neurotic, or near neurotic, responses to contemporary social and political problems."[27]

In other words, our very attitude toward other humans, toward society, and toward reality itself is severely distorted through the holding of incompatible worldviews, of which either one or both are incorrect. Decision making in all fields of endeavor is affected. A unifying mind-brain theory, a theory acceptable to science *and* to the humanities and religion, must be the center point of a unifying worldview, one able to eliminate the war of worldviews within as well as without.

Not only would unifying contradictory belief systems lead to peace *among* human beings by providing agreed-upon basic assumptions about which a meaningful debate could occur; it would also lead to peace *within* human beings—and through this inner peace would emerge a more rational approach to the problems themselves.

Such considerations were in the back of Sperry's mind in 1965 when he laid the foundations of his theory of consciousness as emergent and causal.

> Any model or description that leaves out conscious forces, according to this view, is bound to be sadly incomplete and unsatisfactory. The conscious mind in this scheme, far from being put aside as a by-product, epiphenomenon, or inner aspect, is located front and center, directly in the midst of the causal interplay of cerebral mechanisms. . . . It is a scheme that idealizes ideas and ideals over physical and chemical interactions, nerve impulse traffic, and DNA. It is a brain model in which conscious mental psychic forces are recognized to be the crowning achievement of some five hundred million years or more of evolution.[28]

In 1969, Sperry presented "A Modified Concept of Consciousness," the key paper that concentrated entirely on explaining and defending his new theory.[29] His habit of thinking independently, of fearlessly confronting solidly established assumptions, which had been so successful before, led him to phrase this, his first paper on the subject addressed to an audience of scientists, with appropriate boldness. He flung down the gauntlet, taking issue with what had been a long-established tenet of neuroscience—that consciousness has no effect on physical and chemical activity within the brain.[30]

The challenge worked.

The paper elicited criticism, discussion, and counterstatements by its author, and it had considerable impact. It helped to make efforts to establish the legitimacy of consciousness from other quarters, such as philosophy, psychology, cybernetics, studies of drug effects on the brain, and so on, more effective; and it helped to bring about a swing from a materialist-reductionist-behaviorist worldview to a new view in which consciousness was crucial—in which mind mattered.

Sperry's part in the swing was probably larger than the credit he received for it in the press. His pioneer work had introduced a new concept into the philosophy of science which others used successfully to strengthen their positions. There will have been many who, like Eccles, labored under a disturbing and long-standing dissatisfaction with the materialist-behaviorist treatment of consciousness, but who, unlike Eccles, could neither accept belief in a supernatural directing agency nor find an alternative, scientifically acceptable solution of their own. For these persons, the publication of "A Modified Concept of Consciousness" together with subsequent illuminating discussions about it—all published in the widely read *Psychological Review*—must have seemed like the opening of a long-locked sluice gate, allowing them to pour forth their own ideas and thoughts on the matter.

As for Eccles himself, whose dualist interpretation of the mind-body relationship we discussed in chapter 2, Sperry describes his reaction to this new conception of consciousness in his paper "Mind-Brain Interaction: Mentalism, Yes; Dualism, No." Referring to the Vatican Conference in Rome in 1964 (which Eccles had organized), Sperry reports that, when he suggested that consciousness may have some "operational and causal use," Eccles responded, "Why do we have to be conscious at all? We can, in principle, explain all our input-output performance in terms of activity of neuronal circuits; and consequently, consciousness seems to be absolutely unnecessary."[31] In saying this, Eccles expressed the prevailing point of view among neuroscientists at the time. Interactionist concepts had long been conceived as a "complete heresy," both by scientists and by most philosophers. Those who objected to this unsatisfactory state of affairs were helpless. Eccles, a convinced dualist, went on to add: "I don't believe this story [the irrelevance of consciousness], of course; but at the same time, I do not know the logical answer to it."[32]

Eccles had in 1953 proposed an answer of his own to the mind-brain problem, suggesting that minuscule extraphysical "influences," originating in a different and separate mental world, impinge on individual synapses. His words to Sperry showed how dissatisfied he had become with that solution by 1964. Once introduced to Sperry's concept of downward causation, which involves the *supervenience,* or superimposing, of higher-order natural events onto lower-order ones (and which leaves physical interactions in the brain intact and untouched, instead of presupposing extraphysical "influences" which interfere with neurochemistry), Eccles was now able to revise and considerably strengthen his own interpretation of the mind-brain relationship—although he never renounced the need for a separate mental realm to explain the existence of a self-conscious mind.[33] At first glance, Eccles's final product differs considerably from that of Sperry. Yet it rests on Sperry's formula for mind-brain interaction. In arguing for his position, Eccles acknowledges freely and generously that Sperry had earlier proposed a similar view.[34]

In many other cases, however, the concept of downward causation was incorporated into, and provided strength for, other widely divergent individual theories without special mention—and possibly sometimes even without knowledge—of their origin in Sperry's work. Ideas interacted with one another and led to the production of still newer and different ideas. Though cross-fertilization occurred and is difficult to trace, a thorough study of related fields reveals the subsequent appearance of the new concept in the domain of holism, general systems theory, mind-brain philosophy, and cognitive psychology, among other areas.[35]

To painstakingly trace the progress of emergent causation across the mental landscape is not our primary concern. The important point is this. By 1977, the materialist-reductionist-behaviorist view of the world appeared to be a nightmare of the past, at least in the behavioral sciences, if not in physics. Sperry could state with relief that "it becomes increasingly impossible, among other things, to accept the idea of two separate realms of knowledge, existence, or truth: one for objective science and another for subjective experience and values." He documented the disappearance of "seemingly irreconcilable paradoxes" into a "single continuous hierarchy" as we move upward in the brain from its "subnuclear particles . . . through the atoms, molecules, and brain cells to the level of nerve circuit systems without consciousness, and finally to cerebral processes with consciousness." Such a mental journey, he believed, would erase the science-values dichotomy, as "objective facts and subjective values become parts of the same universe of discourse."[36]

Further Explanation of a Hypothesis

Scientific creation is an act as individual and idiosyncratic as literary creation—a fact too seldom realized by the general public. Sometimes a scientist may burst upon the scene virtually overnight, presenting a theory that even in its earliest form is a masterpiece of cogency and elegance. Einstein's introduction of special relativity in 1905 is a good example. Other theories are developed more gradually, over time and in a series of papers.

Sperry's work on emergent causation seems to fall into the latter category. In a condensed reference list following his autobiography in *Les Prix Nobel, 1981*—the official Nobel Prize publication—Sperry listed only two of his writings on philosophy, both of which treated his mind-brain theory and his philosophy of ethics simultaneously. To this list should be added the earlier key papers: "Mind, Brain and Humanist Values"[37] and "A Modified Concept of Consciousness," which appeared in *Psychological Review* in 1969. The clearest and most lucid explanation of his mind-brain theory, however, is found in a lesser-known paper, "An Objective Approach to Subjective Experience: Further Explanation of a Hypothesis," which was written as a response to the chief critic of the 1969 *Psychological Review* paper, Professor Dalbir Bindra.[38]

Such interchange and interplay of competing ideas is irreplaceable and invaluable. To hold any validity, a theory must be challenged and tested, over and over. Such testing is central to the scientific process, and only through such testing are theories refined and honed so that they become useful tools by which to understand the universe. Each defense of a challenged theory expresses it more concisely and presents it in a clearer light.

In both his 1965 and 1970 papers, Sperry explained that scientists have recognized emergent phenomena outside the brain as causally potent, no matter what the level of organization. Why should consciousness be an exception?[39] The objection that in the case of consciousness one of these levels, that is, brain function, is material, while the other, the level of thoughts and values affecting brain function, is not does not mark consciousness as unique, either; even in a field as hard-edged as engineering, nonmaterial emergent qualities cause material effects, as we shall see later in the book. Besides, the entire field of quantum mechanics, with its constant interaction of material and nonmaterial entities, and with its conversion of matter into energy and vice versa, makes the above objection seem rather irrelevant. A further objection, that Sperry's hypothesis lacks the appropriate level of detail, is well-taken. So does *every* new hypothesis before it becomes accepted fact, especially in a field as complex and relatively unexplored as the mind-brain relation. But, as Sperry himself pointed out, his theory "ought to appear somewhat less vague than alternative theories of mind available to date."[40]

Sperry then proceeded to differentiate his view from other mind-brain theories. One of these, the *inner aspect theory,* holds that the phenomenon of consciousness is merely one aspect of brain processes. Sperry, on the other hand, argued that consciousness is an integral part of brain processes, and "a complete objective description *that included the spatial and temporal pattern features of the neural activity, as such* [italics added], would perforce include the mental properties."[41] By "spatial and temporal pattern features," Sperry meant the holistic properties that emerge from the interaction of billions of individual neurons in the brain. His contention that such holistic properties are not included in standard, reductionistic explanations of nature has led to constant friction with other scientists. He has continued to insist that consciousness cannot be relegated to one corner, as an inconvenient and unimportant minor aspect of brain activity, and that an understanding of holistic properties—whether they be of the brain or of other objects—is crucial to a comprehensive understanding of the natural world.

Another theory with which Sperry took issue is called the *identity theory.* It holds that subjective experience and the neural activities of which it is composed are one and the same. To understand those neural activities, then, is to understand consciousness, which may once again be safely relegated to a corner. But, Sperry pointed out, different neural events can produce the same conscious effect, while identical neural events can produce different conscious effects depending on what context they occur in. He admitted that the identity theory could "conceivably be expanded to include the kind of psychoneural interaction we now envisage, but not without significant changes in its present approach and formulation."[42] In any case, two things or events are identical only if they are identical in all their details. If we accept this criterion, a description of neural events, no matter how exact, that leaves out the conscious phenomena produced by them cannot possibly be considered identical with consciousness.

Although, as Sperry explained, events occurring in each subsystem are controlled by the qualities of the wholes they create—in the brain as well as everywhere else in nature—"the mental phenomena and the physical brain processes are seen to be mutually interdependent. Neither is primary nor ultimate to the exclusion of the other."[43] To understand human beings, one must understand both the content of their thoughts and the physicochemical nature of brain activity.

Sperry pointed out that mere complexity or higher-order neural functions alone are insufficient to produce consciousness. The cerebellum, for instance, displays both but lacks consciousness (as far as we know). It is "the specific operational design of the cerebral mechanism for the particular conscious function involved," that grants conscious awareness to neural events. Such a design is structured to "create particular sensations, perceptions, and feelings, and to provide a rapid representation of external reality."[44]

In responding to Bindra, Sperry expressed his mind-brain philosophy in terms that brought it closest to the framework of scientific thought. But in other writings, he proved himself similarly at ease in providing a lighthearted, humor-filled exposition of his point of view to a nonscientific (or mixed) audience.

> Among other things, the theory holds that most of the atoms on our planet are primarily moved around not by atomic or subatomic laws and forces, as quantum physics would have it, but by laws and forces of classical physics, biology, geology, meteorology, even sociology, politics, and the like. For example, the molecules of higher living things are moved around mostly by the living, vital powers of the particular species in which they're embedded. They're flown through the air, galloped across the plains, swung through the jungle and propelled through the water not by molecular forces or quantum mechanics but by specific holistic, vital, and also mental properties—aims, wants, needs—possessed by the organism in question. Once evolved, the higher laws and forces exert downward control over the lower.[45]

Sperry's strong emphasis—perhaps even overemphasis—on holistic properties may act as a roadblock against the acceptance of his philosophy by scientists, who traditionally have been suspicious of anything that might smack in the least of mysticism.

For nonscientists, the details of his explanations may appear confusing. It is worth stating his main message again, as simply as possible. Although our existence ultimately depends upon events at the micro-level—the interactions of the subatomic particles which are the building blocks of matter—these events have brought forth level over level of new entities, or phenomena, each with new powers, new properties, and new potency, which constantly influence, redirect, and rearrange the relationships among events at lower levels. Laws and phenomena at the micro-level still operate; their overall coordination, however, is determined by the laws and phenomena of higher-level organization.

In contrast to reductionism, such a conception of reality does not destroy or eliminate the most fascinating aspects of life. But it does help explain them.

·5·
Concern with Values

What is needed ideally . . . to make decisions [involving value judgments]
is a consensus on some supreme comprehension and interpretation of the
universe and the place and role within it of man and the life experience.
—Roger Sperry

The Supreme Good

What is the "supreme good"—the ultimate goal of human
striving, effort, and intellect? That is the central question Sperry
addresses in his work on ethics, and it will be our focus in this
and succeeding chapters.

At the core of his philosophy is the conviction that the continued existence of the earth's biosphere—"without which," as
Sperry says, "there is nothing"—is the supreme good around
which human value systems must be organized. Employing
that axiom as a foundation, and recognizing the fact that our
world is dynamic, not static, Sperry goes on to derive an ethical
code that defines morally correct behavior as "that which preserves and enhances the evolving quality of existence."[1]

Inevitably conflicts will arise among different products of evolution struggling for existence, be they organisms or ideas.
How would the proposed ethic help to resolve these conflicts?
Sperry suggests that the choice ought to be made "in terms of
the common good, ultimately in the perspective of the long-
range evolving quality of the biosphere as a whole."[2] In short:
"The grand design of nature" and "the upward thrust of evolution as part of the design become something to preserve and
to revere."[3]

By adopting such an ethic, Sperry believes, we would commit ourselves to progress—not so much material progress as mental and spiritual advancement. "Although the essential importance of the lower level forces is recognized and accepted in the new outlook, priority is given to the higher, more evolved spiritual and idealistic dimensions in the cognitive structure."[4]

Like the French philosopher Pierre Teilhard de Chardin, Sperry considers evolution to be a consistent flow from the less complex to the more complex, and he equates the greatest complexity with the advent of purpose, meaning, and spirituality in the universe, which the forward thrust of evolution is bound to increase.

The truth of science, he believes, must necessarily lead to moral convictions that would support reverence for nature and its essence, creativity,

> including . . . its peak thrust into the highest reaches of man's mind, along with corollary value criteria which, if applied worldwide, would promptly set into motion the kinds of corrective legislation and other trends and pressures that are needed to remedy looming global disaster conditions.[5]

Unlike Teilhard, however, he sees no external or internal guiding intellect directing the process, and he does not share Teilhard's conviction that eventually an *Omega point* will be reached, with evolution culminating in something Teilhard terms the *noosphere,* a level of ultimate spiritual development. Instead, Sperry believes that evolution has no predetermined goal and that nature has no special preference for man.

Moreover, Sperry differs significantly from Teilhard in his views on population pressure. While Teilhard sees the masses of men of the future melting together into one loving community, like atoms being forced together, fusing, and transmuting under the enormous pressures within the core of a young star, Sperry—perhaps benefiting from the insight produced by more extensive experience in the "real" world—sees population increase accompanied by dissent, ruthlessness, and severe degradation of the quality of existence, a degradation, most of all, of spirituality, values, and sense of personal worth.

Accordingly, the supreme good—of which striving toward the preservation and enhancement of the evolving quality of existence is a part—demands that our species adopt a new and more responsible ethic to remain worthy of sharing this planet. Recognition that most of today's problems can already be ascribed to excessive population growth calls for the development of a new system of belief that would "make it sacrilegious to deplete natural resources, to pollute the environment, to over-populate, to erase or degrade other species, or to otherwise destroy, demean, or defile the evolving quality of the biosphere."[6]

Sperry's views about the degrading effects of overpopulation are strongly confirmed by such observations as those related by Langdon Gilkey in his book *Shantung Compound*. His account of life in a Japanese wartime compound describes the slow disintegration of what had been a civilized and well-educated group of persons, mainly missionaries and religiously oriented professors, who in their lives before internment had been committed to the highest standards of ethics. Nonetheless, lack of food and space led at the end to a predominance of greed, avarice, and petty self-centeredness with very few exceptions. "Human nature," we must conclude, is strongly influenced not only by genetic predisposition and education but also by the quality of external living conditions.

Examples like these add to the conviction that facts and values are closely interrelated, a conviction that permeates all of Sperry's thinking and that lies at the basis of his joined interest in mind-brain theory and in values. His mind-brain theory and his philosophy of ethics are, in fact, so intimately related and interconnected that it is difficult to treat both aspects of his work separately. He himself usually combined both in all his papers, merely shifting emphasis either to the mind-brain problem or toward values. In fact, his prolonged, persistent wrestling with the mind-brain problem was motivated in no small part by his inner dissatisfaction with the emptiness of a

purely fact-oriented world and his recognition of how important it is to find a credible way to reinstate meaning and values
into the most influential and most rapidly spreading belief system on earth—that of science. This motivation expressed itself
in relatively early writings and has been sustained throughout
his life. As early as 1952, Sperry maintained that the link between mind and brain is at the heart of metaphysics, and that
truly understanding that link "could have vast influence on all
the ultimate aims and values of mankind."[7]

One must recall that in the 1950s, the heyday of behaviorism,
the very mention of values in a scientific context seemed inadmissible and demanded unusual self-confidence. Sperry's contention, an act of courage and conviction, was repeated and
sharpened in each one of his later papers on the subject. Constantly, he highlighted the connection between our understanding of the mind-brain relationship and our ability to solve
global problems. Contrasting the prevailing reductionistic science—"by nature . . . dehumanizing, destroying values and
meaning"—with the new view that mind and consciousness
supersede biophysical, chemical, and physiological forces, he
pointed out that the first view separated science from value
judgments, while the second allowed "a congenial mergence of
science with the value disciplines." Relying on improved technology and the endless resources of outer space will be less useful, he believed, than a "change of the kind of value systems we
live and govern by." Such a shift provides "the prime hope for
tomorrow's world."[8] Among the advantages of a value system
inspired by a deeper understanding of science would be greater
credibility, an appeal to humanity's spiritual and aesthetic
sense, and the promotion of attitudes and action that would
"counter global trends toward worsening world conditions."[9]

The "real phenomena" of "wholes and their properties" and
"their causal potency"—in short, the principle of downward
causation—is the key concept tying together Sperry's mind-
brain theory and his philosophy of ethics. His idea of consciousness as emergent and causal can be interpreted as one

specific instance of an overarching view of reality. Everywhere in the dynamic, evolving universe unforeseen and unexpected phenomena arise through new combinations of interactions. Each of these phenomena enriches the world with new effects; each is causally active, affecting higher levels of organization by forever bringing forth new, as yet unknown, constellations and shaping lower levels of organization by affecting previously constructed entities. From this welter of dynamic activity, from this wonderful and miraculous occurrence of continuing, emerging causation, Sperry singles out the downward causation of the mind onto brain activity for special attention—a facet of reality that has so far been almost completely neglected by science, and one that is of crucial importance to the future of our species and the biosphere itself. Downward causation is a special instance of emergent causation, and it is the concept of downward causation that provides ethical convictions with their immense power—even in the worldview of science.

Through emergent causation, Sperry does nothing less than open a new field of study—one that must be considered as additional to traditional science and traditional religion, and as partly replacing these. This "new science" centers on the human mind as the crucial interface between objective knowledge and values. It takes into account that all complex, interacting activity remains senseless and without meaning unless it can be understood and explained as being coordinated through a higher-level emergent or a supervening principle. The dynamic quality of life is retained, the powerful impact of mental experience safeguarded.

In our view, the new approach to ethics promises to be immensely fruitful. While science transcends its one-sided preoccupation with numbers and measurements and becomes more oriented toward the needs of humanity, religion's need to search for meaning in an otherworldly realm will be reduced, so that questions of ethics can be discussed in a more accessible framework: our own world of the here and now. Rendered more relevant, religion could then address such issues as pollution, overpopulation, depletion of natural resources, and the threat of nuclear warfare, taking into account both the demands of scientific fact and the necessity of considering human values and needs in finding solutions.

The nature of religion would, of course, change enormously under this new worldview. Humanity's creator could no longer be seen as an unembodied spirit or intellect concerned with the fate of man above everything else. Science and ethics would no longer oppose each other. Thus, it would make sense to ask what are the values we need for the survival of mankind; and once they are found, to promote their acceptance—not as laws decreed by a traditional God whose existence may be doubted, but as laws of nature that cannot be evaded.

These values of which we speak will probably turn out not to differ greatly from those intuitively perceived in previous ages by persons of unusual intelligence, wisdom, and concern. But restated in the context of this new science, they will be subject to winnowing, revision, and updating in the light of increased knowledge.

Now that we have touched on some of the essentials of the system of ethics put forward by Sperry, let us systematically state the major concepts, as they have been set out in his papers, before continuing to examine them in greater detail.

1. Actions that preserve and enhance the evolving quality of existence are ethically good and morally right.
2. A realistic view of the world must include the concept of *downward causation*—that is, the causal potency of emergent holistic laws and properties. Wholes are more than the sums of parts, often in surprisingly unpredictable ways.
3. Values are ordered in logical hierarchies.
4. Facts and values are not strictly separated.
5. Freedom and determinism are compatible with one another.

We have dealt with the first two points in some detail, and will now turn to the last three, beginning with the question of hierarchy.

The Hierarchy of Values

Clinging to absolute values in a changing world where there are no absolutes will inevitably lead to cruelties, degradation, and possibly to the annihilation of mankind itself. To arrive at values that are solid but not unchangeable, sacred but not immovable, Sperry proposes establishing a hierarchy of values, in which one unchanging ultimate axiom determines value judgments at lower levels. Under that conception, lower-level judgments may change, depending on exterior conditions, but will always remain constant in relation to the ultimate aim to be achieved.

What kind of ultimate aim or "superior axiom" do we have in mind? Enlightened, farsighted, and future-oriented concern for the quality of existence is such an ultimate goal. Of course, the specific interpretation of this goal then becomes of crucial importance. Sperry equates reverence for the forward thrust of evolution with this kind of future-oriented thinking. Traditional religion, on the other hand, has emphasized the notion of life after death.

Fiat Justitia et Pereat Mundus (Let Justice be Done Though the World Perish), the motto of the Holy Roman Emperor Ferdinand I (1503–1564), was probably inspired by his belief in a better world beyond the one on earth. To demolish that belief without providing a substitute is no solution. Indeed, Ferdinand's imperative still seems to be very much alive among those who would sacrifice the species for high ideals—while forgetting that all ideals would vanish with it. Clearly, what the world needs are values promoting justice *and* life.

Sperry's work can be interpreted as a search for justice *and* life. He clearly sees that science, while concentrating on facts, illuminates fundamental errors in our belief and value systems which must be adjusted if the goals toward which we strive are to be reached. If the beliefs at the very core of our society are wrong—if they are hopelessly incompatible with a modern understanding of reality—then the social structures built on these beliefs will also be distorted. We will be valiantly trying to do things we shouldn't, while at the same time ignoring tasks vital to our survival. One is reminded of the biblical parable of the house built on sand. And, as Sperry points out in his 1972 paper "Science and the Problem of Values," some of our core beliefs may very well be mistaken; for they were arrived at in a time when most people believed "the world was flat, the sun circled the earth, and the seat of the mind was the liver."[10]

In this paper Sperry presents for the first time his philosophy of ethics in its complete form; he also notes that with the advent of human intelligence, life on earth enters new and uncharted waters. In what has been, by the measure of geological and biological evolution, but an eye-blink of time, the older natural forces that prevailed for eons have been usurped. Now humanity is in charge; and, indeed, perhaps the most astonishing aspect of this moment of earth's long history is "this radical shift in biospheric controls away from the vast interwoven matrix of pluralistic time-tested checks and balances of nature, to the much more arbitrary, monistic, and relatively untested mental capacities and impulses of the human brain."[11]

How can humanity wield its new powers wisely? That is the theme that winds its way through Sperry's work on ethics. He believes that the new conditions under which we live have rendered values too vital to suffer from neglect or "hands-off" policies, as they still generally are in such fields as science, economics, and even psychology.[12] In our quest for future-oriented values, the concept of downward causation, which elevates thought and foresight over more immediately brain-dependent instincts, will be essential in deciding about "what is good, right, and ethically true, and what ought to be."[13]

In some ancient myths, the creator of the universe could be described as an animal possessing supernatural powers without, apparently, arousing disbelief or misgivings in the minds of believers. Later, when the creator became responsible for not just the material world but man's mores, too, only a human being, a mother or father, would do. Later still, the spiritual nature of that being, or of being itself, had to be emphasized to satisfy man's need for logical clarity. Finally, nothing was sufficient. The question itself became taboo, and man arrived at a vacuum that turned life itself into an experience without meaning and purpose. Human nature, however, is not constructed to tolerate chaos or emptiness. Without guidance, disintegration takes place; and, as Sperry notes, "humanity needs to see itself in terms of something more and greater than itself to give meaning and purpose to human existence."[14]

For Sperry, as for many other profound thinkers, the powers of nature, the powers creating and changing the universe, the forces improving living systems, are those most realistically equated with the image of the divine. Such an image finds its roots in the misty dawn of history. An image of something transcending mankind has always been needed to provide a beacon for humanity's highest hopes and aspirations, and the reconciliation of such an ideal with advancing empirical knowledge has been a task that has long attracted the talented and insightful. Sperry is not the only such individual, not even in the present; but his studies of the mind-brain relationship and of downward causation make his work unique and worthy of deeper consideration.

Facts and Values

The need to update religion periodically in the light of increasing knowledge so that it may retain its credibility illustrates another tenet of Sperry's ethical system: facts and values cannot be separated. Science is man's "number one source of factual information," he argues, and "an informed judgment is generally preferable to one that is uninformed or misinformed." Judgments of ethical right and wrong are no exceptions; therefore, he is convinced, "science would seem on this count as well to deserve a leading role in shaping ethical values instead of being disqualified."[15]

The drastic consequences of a refusal to take facts into account cannot be overstated. The biologist Garrett Hardin, using as an example a reindeer population, has shown that failure of foresight in regulating population will catastrophically reduce a species' numbers not just to the level that their habitat would normally support, but to a level far lower still—to remain at that level for centuries to come. Referring to David Klein's classic study of the reindeer on Saint Matthews Island, Hardin reports:

> In 1944 a population of 29 animals was moved to the island, without the corrective feedback (negative feedback) of such predators as wolves and human hunters. In 19 years, the population swelled to 6,000 and then "crashed" in 3 years to a total of 41 females and 1 male, all in miserable condition. Klein estimates that the primeval carrying capacity of the island was about 5 deer per square kilometer. At the population peak there were 18 per square kilometer. After the crash there were only 0.126 animals per square kilometer, *and even this was probably too many* once the island was largely denuded of lichens. Recovery of lichens under zero population condition takes decades and with a continuous resident population of reindeer it may never occur. Transgressing the carrying capacity of St. Matthew Island reduced its carrying capacity by at least 97.5 percent.[16]

Foreseeing a similar long-term threat in human overpopulation, Sperry insists on values based on facts and foresight. It is not enough to wait until the crisis is upon us, hoping that imminent catastrophe will force a realignment of our values into more acceptable, favorable, and survivable patterns. That sort of procrastination would leave us "doomed always to live on the margins of tolerability, because only if things begin to get intolerable does the voting majority get around to changing established values."[17]

Insistence on the close interrelationship between facts and

values has been a component of emergent causation from its very beginnings. Sperry's first public mention of that relationship occurred in 1964 during his lecture at the American Museum of Natural History in New York, in which he maintained that reliable information about how the mind and brain are related, and about the precise nature of consciousness—not to mention all that such information would imply—could shake up our culture's dominant values and beliefs.[18]

In 1965, he expressed his disagreement with the assumption that scientists must not and cannot apply knowledge and insights derived through their profession to the discussion of value problems. Such a belief would support, he points out, the notion that "value judgments lie outside of the realm of knowledge and understanding," that "the best method we know of applying the human brain to problems of understanding must be discarded when it comes to problems of values," and that "science is able to deal only with those phenomena and products of evolution that appeared prior to the emergence of higher brains . . . and, of course, the corresponding value systems that these impose."[19] He is convinced, and we share that conviction, that "values have natural and logical origins."

In his key 1972 paper on values, Sperry drew attention to the relationship between science, values, and social conditions, a theme he treated with increasing urgency in later papers. "Should humankind put its faith in the kind of truth within which scientific and religious belief are in accord, or should we continue to reach beyond this realm into others of less certainty?" he asked in 1988. We must remain "firmly within the realm of empirical verification," he asserted, declaring that "if civilization is to survive and continue on a forward course. . . . We can no longer afford the risk of mistakes in this critical area."[20] Science did not create our present dilemma; instead, Sperry believes, it is our values that have proved inadequate and that have misdirected the application of science to technological and social problems.[21]

According to Sperry, the effect of the merging of science and values, and the knowledge that our creator is identical with the creative forces that produced the "Grand Design of Nature," would not change the essentials of any one religion's contributions to humanity but would purify and enhance their influence by eliminating detrimental "fringe differences." The new system of belief would share a great deal with already established faiths. But how it diverges from them would mean all the difference in confronting the disasters now threatening our world; for "ancient taboos, mythical beliefs, and a variety of cultural traditions, barbarisms, and sacred cows" would be swept away, replaced by strategies to deal with such things as the regulation of pollution and population, the degradation of the biosphere, human conflict, the rights of nonhuman species, and many other issues.[22]

A complete understanding of the relationships among evolution, brain function, behavior, and cultural influences on behavior leads to the conclusion that individuals with values not conducive to human survival have been continuously eliminated, first through death and later through the adjustment of their theories to prevailing and stubborn facts. The well-known and influential philosopher Karl Popper describes the process succinctly:

> On the pre-scientific level, we are often ourselves destroyed, eliminated, with our false theories; we perish with our false theories. On the scientific level, we systematically try to eliminate our false theories—we try to let our false theories die in our stead.[23]

Innumerable treatises of philosophy have been written on the fact-value question, disregarding this point. From a larger perspective, however—from the perspective of a yet-to-be-established new science—it becomes apparent that a worldview constructed from the limited amount of knowledge we have so far been able to establish scientifically is not satisfactory, nor is a worldview excluding that knowledge in the name of religious truth, nor one demanding the strict separation of two kinds of incompatible truths. All of these views belong to those "false theories" we must let "die in our stead." To be viable, a view of the world would have to merge key aspects of both.

Jacques Monod warned that a merging of science and values would destroy science. In creating a new science along the lines described above, however, his warning does not apply. Science is not being changed to accommodate the values of a preconceived orthodoxy, as happened in the Middle Ages. Instead, values are adjusted to take account of well-winnowed scientific knowledge in order to achieve ethical goals which cannot be reached in any other way. Unlike Monod, Sperry sees mankind's supreme aim not as the accumulation of objective knowledge in and for itself, but as the gathering of knowledge relevant to an ultimate value, that value being determined by man's inner ethical experience.

Sperry is not alone in such a conviction. Nicholas Maxwell, a British historian and philosopher of science, has argued that the aim of contemporary "standard empiricism"—usually expressed as the need to improve our knowledge of "value-neutral factual truth"—is woefully insufficient. In fact, if we adhere to a rigid definition of standard empiricism, we would have to exclude the consideration of the aims and purpose of science from the realm of scientific thought, as something not fitting the criterion of "value-neutral factual truth"! "In fact, however," writes Maxwell, "science does not seek to increase our knowledge of factual truth as such, but out knowledge of *important* factual truth, truth that we deem to be in some way valuable, significant, interesting, beautiful, useful, from either a cultural or a practical technological standpoint." Therefore, Maxwell argues, science must incorporate not only contributions at the level of experiment and theory but also those that "articulate, explore and criticise possible aims for science," and he even suggests that a Nobel Prize should be given not only for direct *contributions* to science but also for enlightening the world about the *most desirable direction* science ought to take. The "best aims for science," he believes, "lie in the direction of the overlap between that which is scientifically realisable, and that which is humanly desirable."[24] Indeed, Maxwell illuminates the significance of Sperry's endeavors from a new direction. Providing science with a new and worthwhile aim may turn out to be Sperry's greatest contribution.

Nevertheless, neither Sperry nor Monod, and of course not Maxwell, would go as far as to argue that the *ultimate* value we need could be found through objective science alone. *That* value must be accepted as an axiom—a gift of intuitive insight.

Even with that qualification, Sperry's contention that science "accept . . . within its causal domain the whole world of inner experience"[25] will seem just as awkward and contradictory as Stoic talk about a "universal city" to those who define science as that which can be subjected to mathematical manipulation, and who know that science's extraordinary progress has been a result of working within that limitation. The word *science* in the sense Sperry uses it will eventually have to be replaced by something more comprehensive. But the idea itself, struggling to be expressed—the notion of a wider, more inclusive science—is just as valid as Galileo's "fixed stars that move" and as promising as the Stoics' "faintly perceived notion" of a single worldwide society.[26]

Free Will

How can the scientific perception of reality as a tightly woven matrix of cause-effect relationships be reconciled with the pervasive subjective experience that we are free to choose?

At one time it was thought that quantum mechanics, through the discovery of the uncertainty principle and the application of that principle to brain function, would provide an escape from the unending chain of cause and effect relationships that must be found in the decision-making processes of the brain. Thus the idea of free will might be rescued. The uncertainty principle holds that there is a certain "graininess" or "fuzziness" inherent in our observations of the universe; measurements of energy, position, and motion of subatomic particles can never be completely precise, because the very act of observing affects what is being observed. At best, at the subatomic level, we can speak only of the statistical likelihood of an event occurring, not hard-edged cause and effect. Building on this foundation, some philosophers have argued that the uncertainty principle introduces a certain measure of chance into the way in which the brain makes decisions.

Such hopes were dashed, however, on further reflection. For one thing it seemed that the uncertainty principle would produce in the brain not freedom from constraint but, more likely, sheer chaos. For another, the interactions that produce consciousness operate at the level of the cell and larger still, far above the level at which the weird statistical worldview of quantum mechanics supersedes the "common sense" reality of what might be called the *macroworld*. Insight into the behavior of quantum particles cannot help us explain the existence of freedom.

The theory of emergent causation, however, leads naturally to the insight that the coexistence of freedom and determinism is not only possible but *necessary.* Sperry's changed concept of consciousness casts the determinism versus free will debate in a new light. Our definitions of both are crucially changed, and the result is a new answer which includes and integrates elements of both determinism and free will—but redefined and conceived differently.

As consciousness emerges from brain activity, it is intimately connected with the subjective experience of freedom. There is no question we *feel* free. But the real issue we must explore is not experience of freedom but the problem of whether that feeling is just an illusion. Are we really free? And can emergent causation help answer that age-old puzzle?

What I do by free choice is not uncaused but determined by *what I want to do.* The true cause of my actions resides not in the random movements of quantum particles but in my own thoughts and values. From the viewpoint of emergent causation, we can define determinism in an entirely new way—

though originating at the atomic level, it has been thoroughly transformed during its passage through several successive levels of emergence, so that it has become an entirely different process when operating in the macroworld. If I have mental wants, I do what I want to do—but what I choose to do is *not* uncaused. In a way, the idea of cosmic fatalism is retained; the universe is lawful, *everything* in it is caused, and we can justifiably hope that science will find many (if not all) of these causes and explain them. Such a perception of reality is much better than having an *un*caused and therefore unpredictable, unreliable, and even meaningless universe.

Reconciling freedom and determinism is a major strength of Sperry's theory. The scientific view that brain and behavior are determined—that all events have their causes—is maintained; but the traditional mechanistic, physicochemical type of determinism, which traces macroscopic effects back to microscopic causes, is profoundly transformed. Cognitive and mental phenomena that cannot be reduced to subatomic or subnuclear components are now recognized as causes of how we act and behave.

As we think, the pattern of brain events and associated thoughts proceeds in a lawful, causally determined manner. Otherwise no rational response to unforeseen circumstances could be made, no long range planning could occur, no sensible choices in difficult situations would be possible. This is the level at which the experience of freedom arises and becomes a powerful factor in our decision making. Convinced that we have no free will, convinced that we are in the thrall of forces beyond our control or even our understanding, we could easily be zombies or automatons. But if, under the very same external circumstances, the inner feeling of freedom is present, we are inspired, liberated, and we discover unsuspected wellsprings of inner strength.

Of all the causal factors produced by our subjective experiences, this inner sense of freedom is surely one of the most crucial.

Throughout his papers on philosophy, Sperry discusses, and sheds light on, the freedom-determinism controversy. The explanation we prefer above all others, however, is his very first illumination of the problem during a 1964 lecture at the American Museum of Natural History in New York, which displays a light touch and a genuine sense of humor.

Here, Sperry speaks of free will as an "evolved emergent property of the brain that appeared between man and higher apes, or, depending on whom you read, maybe somewhere after bacteria perhaps, but before houseflies." He deplores the exclusion of free will from the worldview of the behavioral sciences (though *mind* and *consciousness* were beginning to return to respectability), and set out to remedy matters. Of course, no tool could be better suited for this purpose than the concept of downward causation, expressed here for the first time, ingeniously camouflaged in order to disarm initial objections and yet containing a powerful and ultimately victorious core.

> A molecule in many respects is the master of its inner atoms and electrons [which] are hauled and forced about in chemical interactions by the over-all configurational properties of the whole molecule. . . . If our given molecule is itself part of a single-celled organism such as paramecium, it in turn is obliged . . . to follow along a trail of events in time and space determined largely by the extrinsic over-all dynamics of *Paramecium caudatum*. When it comes to brains, remember that the simpler electric, atomic, molecular, and cellular forces and laws, though still present and operating, have been superseded by the configurational forces of higher-level mechanisms. . . . In the human brain, these include the powers of perception, cognition, reason, judgment, and the like.[27]

Envisioning the human brain as an intricately intertwined component of "the causal flow of cosmic forces," Sperry suggests that it may be far more satisfactory to be one with such a "cosmic flow" than have human behavior occur at random, divorced from cause and effect, immune to any rational explanation or forecast.

——————————————— *Concern with Values* ———————————————

In fact, he speculates, if one were to devise a "perfect free-will model"—the ultimate "decision-making machine"—wouldn't one immerse that machine in all the relevant information it needed, letting it range as widely as possible? And haven't our brains evolved in just that fashion? Our memories furnish us with the fruits of our life experiences; and the invention of writing and printing allow us to tap the wisdom of the ages. Building on this, we can extrapolate future trends.

Perhaps the product, he muses, does not quite meet the ideal

> of universal causal contact; maybe it is not even quite up to the kind of thing evolution has going for itself over on Galaxy Nine; and maybe, in spite of it all, any decision that comes out is still predetermined. Nevertheless, it still represents a very long jump in the direction of freedom from the primeval slime mold, the Jurassic sand dollar, or even the latest model orangutan.[28]

In conclusion: The subjective experience of freedom is produced by various events occurring in the brain. In other words, it is an "emergent product" of these events. Brain activity generates it; yet the experience of freedom also generates brain activity. It has *nothing* to do with a suspension or lapse in cause-effect relationships, nor with the uncertainty principle, which operates at much lower levels. Moreover, the experience that we are free to do what *we* want to do, that we are not being manipulated by what others force upon us, is what matters. *That* is what endows freedom with the high value attributed to it. We need not think of genetic predispositions or the effects of experience on the brain while we act. In fact, to make the fullest use of our potentials, it is better *not* to be distracted by such limitations. We never know what thoughts and ideas may emerge from the various combinations of influences on our brain activity; and the experience of full freedom is one of the most influential factors in the creative process.

The sense of freedom, however illusory, is not merely another link in the chain of causal events. It is an *essential* link. It is the link that makes the entire world of higher mental phenomena

effective. In the worldview we have been describing mind matters; and it matters because it embodies the experience of being
free to perceive, conceive, and create.

Values from Science

Sperry has repeatedly stressed that he was led into the field
of values—which he now considers of greater importance than
his purely scientific work—from and through his preoccupation with science, and not the reverse. His concern with values
stemmed from his concern with the mind-brain problem and
the nature of consciousness. With the emergence of the most
important phenomena of life—consciousness, thought, and
foresight—we can no longer eliminate the influence of human
values from our view of the world. The chasm between the
worldview of science and that of religion—and its dangers—
will vanish, Sperry believes, if we adopt a view of reality that
integrates facts and values into a natural hierarchy.

The theory of emergent causation describes reality as a succession of emergent, and causally active, wholes, all of them
simultaneously parts of a still larger whole. The process does
not cease at the level of individual consciousness. Each individual is part of humankind, and humankind, in turn, is part of
the global ecosystem. Here the theory of emergent causation
connects to ethics. If we feel ourselves part of the natural world
which created us, we become more sensitive to our creator's
directives as well as to our own responsibilities in furthering
and directing evolution's future progress.

Viewed this way, evolution is no longer an enemy of faith; it
is the source of religious experience. If that experience can be
disengaged from its reliance on supernatural powers and joined
to a new concern for our fragile and endangered biosphere, we
will be able to look with renewed hope into the future. Endowed with the unique gift of purpose we are no longer adrift,
carried by forces beyond our control toward an unknown fate,
whether it be degradation or utter extinction. Instead, under-

standing the legacy long eons of evolution have bequeathed to us, we are able to decide on our goals as a species and steer toward them.

Reflections

Perhaps we should pause to briefly sum up the issues we have discussed so far. Coming to philosophy from a lifetime of neuroscience, Roger Sperry looks at the chasm between science and values from a larger perspective and recognizes the outlines of a unifying worldview. He sees mankind as embedded in the web of nature, created through its forces and creating through them; and he sees, beyond mankind, the continued existence of the cosmos at large and our planet's biosphere in particular as a supreme good. These, the sources of our very being and further evolution, the creators of our sense of "right" and "wrong," of our awe of the sacred and divine, demand that we preserve and enhance the evolving quality of existence. Our creator, conceived as "God" by religion, is recognized as being identical with the "forces of nature" as understood by science. That new conception adds potency to the image of a superior power: whether or not we believe in them, we cannot—except at our peril—disobey the laws of nature.

The insight that facts and values cannot be separated is therefore central to Sperry's thoughts on ethics.

His encompassing vision leads to the axiom or *self-evident truth*, which is crucial to his philosophy: the process of evolution from simple to complicated, from lava to living things, from pebbles to people, is something inherently good which must be advanced still further. Basic to that vision, and profoundly influencing his ideas, are the concepts of *emergence* and *downward causation*. Emergence means the appearance of new laws and properties through the combination of parts into wholes. Downward causation is the influence of these newly emergent laws and properties upon all previous creation, including the parts that created the new whole and its never-before-existing powers.

The most significant example of emergent causation is the emergence of consciousness from brain activity and its influence on processes within the brain, and subsequently upon human actions, human history, and, ultimately, upon the fate of the earth.

Sperry's philosophy seeks to reinstate values, meaning, and purpose into a scientific understanding of nature and of life. It would promote striving for an improved quality of existence, and it would embody, according to Sperry's own interpretation, a strong reverence for nature and for the highest spiritual experiences of the human mind. Most importantly, it would provide a basis for intelligible debates to replace unproductive shouting matches between mutually incomprehensible systems of belief. And in that dialogue—and *only* in that dialogue—lies hope for the future.

·6·
Reception of
a Paradigm

The reception of a new paradigm often necessitates a redefinition of the corresponding science. Some old problems may be relegated to another science or declared entirely "unscientific." Others, that were previously non-existent or trivial may, with a new paradigm, become the very archetypes of scientific achievement.

—Thomas Kuhn

Needless to say, Roger Sperry's philosophical ideas have been widely criticized and condemned. Most critics of Sperry's work share an inability to look at his thoughts from a larger perspective, from the point of view of a *new science,* from within a *new realm of understanding* that emphasizes not merely faculty-oriented or even subject-oriented priorities but the priorities of mankind as a whole—and beyond that of life as a whole.

Those who do achieve that wider perspective have generally restricted their criticism to the removal of roadblocks from his way: "I consider Sperry's work of overwhelming significance. My few reservations are the merest nitpicking."[1] These words, for instance, are the reaction of M. E. Grenander, professor of English at the State University of New York at Albany, to Sperry's *Science and Moral Priority.* Grenander is the author of numerous essays on the interface between science and the humanities, and Sperry's ideas may have proved easier to grasp for her than for others.

Without previous preoccupation with the subject, such understanding is more difficult. The situation is best described by Thomas S. Kuhn in his *Structure of Scientific Revolutions*.

> The transition from a paradigm in crisis to a new one from which a new tradition of normal science can emerge is far from a cumulative process, one achieved from an articulation or extension of the old paradigm. Rather, it is a reconstruction of the field from new fundamentals, a reconstruction that changes some of the field's most elementary theoretical generalizations as well as many of its paradigm methods and applications. It involves handling the same problems as before, but placing them in a new system of relations with one another by giving them a new framework.[2]

The study of Kuhn's work leads to one important conclusion: solutions that are obvious from within the framework of a new paradigm may be invisible, or appear wrong, from within the framework of a previous one.

Why Do Distinguished Scientists Do It?

One typical complaint voiced by many critics of Sperry's work is the exasperated exclamation: "Why do distinguished scientists do it?" "It" is concern with global questions, with matters of ethics and values, with problems lying beyond the boundaries of traditional science. And the list of distinguished scientists accused of that crime is indeed long. The framework from within which this exasperation appears valid is one that demands a strict separation of science and values. The critic may be a scientist who (in the words of another reviewer of Sperry's book) "cannot help looking back with nostalgia to the days when Sperry's concerns were with more practical matters,"[3] or he may be a philosopher, convinced that *is* and *ought* must be strictly separated, and deploring the fact that Sperry has disregarded philosophical arguments that it is impossible to reconcile science and values—all the while himself ignoring virtually everything ever written by biologists and others concerned with the human future explaining why—in the interest of our continued existence—it *must* be done.

Sperry's most serious crime, in the eyes of these critics, seems to be that he looks at values *from the vantage point of a scientist* and not merely from that of a human being who also happens to be involved in scientific research. An example of the latter is Nobel laureate Max Delbruck, the pioneer of molecular biology, who said during an interview in 1980:

> I guess one would like to know more where really our values come from. And so you can ask where do the values come from, and you can ask what should our values be, and if you have an answer to what our values *should* be, how to get them to be our values? These are not questions of science, but they are questions the answer to which will decide the further course of history more than anything else. I think the further course of history will not be decided by further discoveries in science, but by these questions of human values.[4]

Here is an eminent scientist who also asks questions about values, but who has at least had the conventional good sense to keep the realm of science strictly separated from the realm of values. The crucial point, however, is that those scientists who have crossed the line—who have merged science and values— have indeed asked themselves "where do our values come from?" and have discovered that the answers lead back to the nature of the human brain and from there to the evolution of life itself—issues well within the domain of science.

Another eminent scientist and Nobel laureate who believed that science and values must remain strictly separated was Jacques Monod; but because he nevertheless proceeded to pronounce objective knowledge as the highest value mankind ought to aspire to, he is listed by Sperry's critics as one of those scientists who "do it." The strictly reductionistic universe of Monod, however, remains cold and empty; there is no place in it for care and concern, no place for the depth of subjective sentiments brought forth through relations of man to man or of man to nature, no place for the spiritual encounter of the divine. Our values, the gift of evolution that made us human, must vanish.

Sperry recognizes the insufficiency of such a worldview; and thus his universe looks different from that of Monod. Emergent causation allows into our conception of reality all the laws and properties brought into being through higher levels of organization. Purpose and meaning, joy and sadness, become part of our world; they become active, effective, causative factors.

This philosophy suggests a solution for the science-value dichotomy that demands neither the neglect or distortion of scientific discoveries to comply with a preconceived absolute value system nor the replacement of values by a reductionistic science rebuilding the world from an incomplete reservoir of factual knowledge—leaving out not only the as-yet-unexplored but everything that cannot be measured or counted. Instead, science is elevated to recognize and incorporate the realities of life.

For the first time, science is given a dignity it has not possessed before. In Sperry's own words:

> So long as science disclaims and rejects the entire realm of inner subjective experience as being acausal, the content and world view of science remain inadequate and unsatisfying for answers that involve subjective value. With the acceptance of a causal concept of conscious experience, the qualitative subjective dimensions in value systems no longer exclude a scientific approach; nor are these subjective dimensions necessarily neglected or demeaned. The scientific image of man regains much of the freedom, dignity, and other humanistic attributes of which it has long been deprived.[5]

Many objections to Sperry's solution involve the argument that a revised science—a science leaving its secure anchorage in facts, numbers, and measurements; a science forsaking reliance on proven knowledge alone—would with that step also give up the power that brought science to its zenith, which is the reliability that made space travel and other feats of progress possible. That argument is well founded.

In fact, upon first encountering Sperry's work, one reacts: "What a magnificent worldview! How immensely important for mankind! But it is not science. It can never be accepted by science without destroying its very foundations. Sperry must change his approach; he must rename his philosophy; he must be brought to recognize that he has discovered something far more important than science itself." And, as one further reflects on the nature of the relationship between science and human concerns, one realizes that the very striving for more and more precision and objectivity that makes science triumphant simultaneously makes it less and less relevant to the most important questions facing humanity; and one sees that ultimate precision and objectivity would lead into the abyss. Indeed, this book's senior author once suggested to Sperry that he adopt the term *new realm of understanding* for his worldview to point out that it is a worldview in which a "revised science" (a science recognizing human needs) and a "revised religion" (a moving spiritual experience of the creative aspect of nature which incorporates scientific truth but is not restricted by it) are able to merge. Traditional science and traditional religion would then retain their previous roles for specific purposes, or specific personal needs. Moreover, the new name would ease the acceptance of the theory of emergent causation in both the religious and the scientific camps, would reduce fears of the destruction of either and thus lessen rejection, and would signal that a new level of knowledge has been reached, inviting mental pioneers to explore its territory.

While most of his critics deplore Sperry's efforts to merge science and values, a few persons share and support them, and some of these persons have arrived through different routes at a conviction that science and values cannot remain separated.

Dr. Ralph W. Burhoe, for instance, came from a devoutly religious background, but he found himself attracted to science and studied astronomy. He grew alarmed and disturbed be-

cause the progress of science seemed linked to the disappearance of values from our society and their replacement by the
shallow, egocentric attitudes of aimless men and women adrift
in a meaningless universe—the "hollow men" of whom T. S.
Eliot wrote. Although convinced of the validity of scientific arguments and the unique expediency of the scientific method,
Burhoe believes that values are essential. Human beings depend on culture, he argues, and humanity is actually a "symbi-
ont" between "ape-man and culture." Neither can exist without
the other. In 1954, together with some friends, he founded the
Institute on Religion in an Age of Science and initiated dialogues between scientists and religious leaders in an effort to
update religion and restore its former credibility. In 1980 he
received for his efforts the prestigious Templeton Prize, the
highest prize awarded for progress in religion. Not surprisingly,
Burhoe supports and endorses Sperry's philosophy.

Another prestigious person convinced that facts and values
are closely related is Dr. Jonas Salk, discoverer of the Salk polio
vaccine and founding director of the Salk Institute. Despite his
scientific fame, he, too, discovered that explorations in that direction form but one element of what the human mind is capable of, and that vast untapped potentialities remain to be developed through a merging of intuition and reason. For Salk, the
survival and further evolution of humanity depend upon
changing our present reliance on brute force in international
affairs to a new reliance on wisdom. He believes that the best
use of his ingenuity lies in helping to develop a "critical mass"
of individuals able to redirect man's attitudes from the pursuit
of shortsighted, destructive aims to that of farsighted, encompassing, and constructive goals.

Why do distinguished scientists do it? Why do they add additional chores to an already overwhelming workload? Why do
they bury themselves beneath this burden and lie awake thinking at night about near-impossible tasks—most often at an age
where other members of society are fully satisfied with a mug
of beer, a game of cards, and a few hours of TV to fill their days?

Why? Because they advance farther into unknown territory than the rest of mankind. They discover new relationships and events unknown to us, and they see dangers of which we are unaware. And why do they care? Because they don't stop being human beings while practicing science; because their love and concern transcend the narrow bounds we have so far been taught to consider; because they know that beyond friends and relatives, beyond all of humanity, beyond reality itself as far as we comprehend it, as long as life and breath and consciousness exist, there will always be a new realm of understanding, a new revelation, a new way of seeing, more profound than anything we have achieved before—more profound than anything we can at present imagine.

"Whatever Is, Is Right"

All Nature is but Art, unknown to thee;
All chance, Direction which thou canst not see;
All Discord, Harmony not understood;
All partial Evil, universal Good:
And spight of Pride, in erring Reason's spight,
One Truth is clear; "Whatever is, is Right."
—Alexander Pope

Needless to say, as we look more closely at Sperry's ethical theory, we see new levels of complication. For one thing, if we accept the Grand Design of Nature as the scientific equivalent of God, does that mean we must also accept a new, revised, and improved version of the argument Alexander Pope and others made in the eighteenth century—that since God represents perfection and God created everything, therefore everything is good? In other words, "whatever is, is right." Or, in terms of Sperry's ethics, does the Grand Design of Nature endorse *everything,* making "all partial evil universal good" in the wider scheme of things?

Or is the "upward thrust of evolution," which Sperry installed as a centerpiece of his theory, nothing more than a mirage?

"Nature is blind and impartial." "The Grand Design of Nature as our creator encourages evil as well and as vigorously as good, and the upward thrust of evolution cannot be discerned in any objective way." These and similar arguments against Sperry's ethics, expressed frequently, not only in published reviews but also by students in his psychobiology class, seem to carry a good deal of weight.

There is also the argument, used by Sperry as well as many other scientists and biologists, that increasing complexity of organization is somehow preferable to simplicity. We find something thoroughly dissatisfying about this. On what grounds could an uninvolved observer possibly judge complexity as better than simplicity? Why should he consider life more precious than inert matter just because it is more complex? Why prefer complex conscious beings over, say, paramecia? And how, in all the world, could it be proved that the human ability to self-reflect has to be valued above the instinct-driven acts and emotions of lower animals? Humans cannot possibly be valued as superior *just because they are more complex!*

But that is, in truth, not why we value them more highly. We value humankind as the apex of evolution because we know a great deal about the *content* of our conscious experience, and that knowledge we could not possibly have gathered through strict adherence to the scientific ideal of objectivity, through the exclusion of all conscious awareness. Moreover, we know—tacitly or intuitively, because there is no other way—that the content of our consciousness is in part shared by other individuals, yet in such innumerable variations that no two minds are alike; and we know, too, that the greater a person's emotional sensitivity and wisdom, the greater is his capacity for empathy and his regard for humanity.

A visitor from outer space, embarking upon an objective inventory of conditions on earth, could not possibly gain any insight into our reality unless he also gained insight into the content of our consciousness. Otherwise he would have to be satisfied with an insufficient and distorted view of the world, as so many human beings dedicated to pure objectivity have been and still are.

In short: From a preparadigm perspective—from the point of view of traditional science, philosophy, or religion—the Grand Design of Nature, with its "upward thrust of evolution," is completely useless as a guiding principle. From the point of view of the new paradigm, however, from within a new science that conceives consciousness, values, and ideals as overwhelmingly important factors in our biosphere, there is no question that an upward thrust of evolution exists. That thrust, however, cannot be explained simply as a development from less complex to more complex structures, although these are generally involved.

Sperry has noted that not complexity itself but specificity of organization is the hallmark of consciousness. The cerebellum may be as complex as the cerebrum or more so, yet it does not produce awareness. *Not* complexity but specific organizational characteristics determine the outstanding features of the new function. Yet even these characteristics, alone, remain meaningless to us unless the emergent they produce, consciousness, becomes known to us. At a level below consciousness, nothing at all can be perceived as meaningful or as good. But as consciousness is reached, value judgments become an inseparable part of our reality system. In fact, they become causal agents of such power that for many human beings death may be preferable to a meaningless, senseless life, or to depravity. Actual examples of self-sacrifice and self-torture caused by belief in a strong, indeed overriding, ideology are too common to require elaboration. We need think only of the millions who have died for the mother country, the fatherland, the church, the state.

As William N. Dember once observed:

> The ideological convert is captured by his ideology; it is not just dominating, it is also pervasive, persistent, and insatiable. Unlike

ordinary motives, which are cyclic, ideology is constant, and instead of being reduced by consummatory activity, it is either un-
affected, or perhaps even enhanced.[6]

In other words, the convert, whether to a political ideology
or to a religious faith, will often make everything else subser-
vient to the cause. In psychological terms, consciousness has
the capacity to supersede the lower-level demands of the autonomous nervous system.

The view of human consciousness as the highest product of
evolution is wholeheartedly endorsed by the most profound
thinkers of past and present the world over. As the well-known
and influential philosopher Michael Polanyi once claimed, "It
is the height of intellectual perversion to renounce, in the name
of scientific objectivity, our position as the highest form of life
on earth."[7] Or, as the philosopher Pascal declared, "All bodies,
the firmament, the stars, the earth and its kingdoms, are not
equal to the lowest mind; for mind knows all these and itself;
and those bodies nothing."[8]

It must therefore be assumed that a visitor from outer space—
once conditions of earth became *completely* known to him, the
content of human consciousness as well as externally observable facts—could not see evolution other than in terms of a progression from lower to higher accomplishments.

Having established that the idea of a forward thrust of evolution is acceptable, the question remains whether, and how,
practical value judgments can be made within such a framework. Again, no sensible answer can be found unless the content of human consciousness is made an active agent in our
conception of reality.

Coming back to Pope's contention that "whatever is, is
right," it is a fundamental mistake to equate reverence for the
forward thrust of evolution with the belief that everything that
has evolved must be good, as proven by its ability to survive.
First of all, over 99 percent of all species that have ever evolved
succumbed to changes in their environment. What is good for

one species, therefore, may be definitely unsuited for another one. Likewise for any particular species one situation might be good, while another might not. The importance of that lesson cannot be emphasized enough.

Our gift of foresight is limited, but it vastly exceeds that of all previous creations of nature, and it must be used and extended as far as possible. Most importantly, we must *incessantly* remain sensitive to the need to change our guidelines for behavior as circumstances warrant. Furthermore, the forward thrust of evolution has now created marvelous visions and ideals in the human mind, such as the worldwide longing for justice. These visions and ideals, according to Sperry's own philosophy of emergent causation, become causal factors in the ongoing process of evolution. They change evolving nature, just as the evolution of the sense of pleasure and pain changed our world in the past, and as the evolution of foresight will become an increasingly potent factor for change in the future. Moreover, visions compete. They force us to ask questions of right and wrong *independently* of the forward thrust of evolution. Which of our visions should be encouraged? Which of them are realistically attainable, which are mere mirages? Under which conditions can justice become a realistic possibility?

Trying to go beyond his original definition of the forces involved in the creation of the Grand Design of Nature as equivalent to God,[9] Sperry sharpened and refined his point of view on ethics. In 1988, still perceiving the cosmos and our planet's biosphere as a "supreme good," he specified as the guiding principle for our determination of right and wrong not merely the upward thrust of evolution as such but "that which preserves and enhances the evolving quality of existence."[10] With that qualification the place for subjective judgment of sentient beings in the process of evolution became more apparent.

Endless arguments, of course, about what constitutes "quality of existence" are possible. Entire university courses have been devoted to defining the term *quality of life.*[11] For Sperry, however, the term is self-explanatory; everyone knows what it means.[12] Careful study of Sperry's work and discussions with him reveal his understanding of "quality of existence" as involving responsibility for the maintenance of an ecological balance, from which not all hardships, not all competition, is eliminated. Humankind itself cannot, and must not, be favored at the expense of that balance. Although he grants that excessive competition will lead to the destruction of our species, he is convinced that competition plays an effective role in many ways in the upward thrust of evolution.

Lewis Mumford argues in his *Transformations of Man* that human ingenuity began to improve the quality of life when human beings began to think of themselves as *separate* individuals, rather than as identical with their community.[13] Persons diverging from accepted norms, including pioneering inventors and thinkers, have been since antiquity (and in some parts of the world are still even now) persecuted or expelled from their tribes as being possessed by evil spirits.[14] The unqualified value of cooperation may be questioned for other reasons. To cooperate with evil, for instance, as often demanded by excessive nationalism, is always wrong.

Sperry also believes we can be too altruistic. He fears a serious lowering of living standards worldwide if the incentive to work and to excel is removed. Most importantly, altruism in excess, and concentrated on *immediate* remedies, would deplete our earth and subject our descendants to squalor and suffering. As the biologist Charles Birch and the process theologian John B. Cobb point out in their *Liberation of Life*, "A society which seeks only justice without regard to its consequences cannot be just. It is unjust to many generations yet unborn."[15] Regard for the future of our earth and of humankind is a constant component of Sperry's conception of justice; it is, in fact, *the* outstanding feature of his global ethic. Every decision he makes for himself or for others is dominated by the thought, often expressed verbally or in letters to his friends: "What difference will it make for our future?"

Sperry's pursuit of the "quality of existence," therefore, involves not so much the removal of hardships as the acceptance of responsibility.

One might interpret "quality of existence" in primarily material terms. Yet, Sperry himself continuously emphasizes the meaningfulness of inner experience as something transcending other measurements of progress. Spirituality, for him, is the mark of man's superiority. In his book *Science and Moral Priority* he quotes Wordsworth in attempting to express his own thoughts on ethics:

> For I have learned
> To look on nature, not as in the hour
> Of thoughtless youth; but hearing oftentimes
> The still sad music of humanity,
> Nor harsh nor grating, though of ample power
> To chasten and subdue.

For Sperry, the struggle between good and evil in individual men and in mankind must be accepted as an inevitable part of the struggle of nature. Yet such a struggle achieves epic proportions as its inevitability is *perceived;* as man learns that his desire to overcome natural limitations is unattainable, and yet that it will never cease to be at the very core of his humanity.

Neither a ceaseless striving for material progress, nor Monod's "anxious quest" for empirical knowledge, but something far greater must guide us onward.

·7·

In Search of
Reference Points

Futurists and common sense concur that a substantial change, world-wide, in life-style and moral guidelines will soon become an absolute necessity.   —Roger Sperry

Peace. Food. No more people than the earth can take. That is the cause.
                                        —C. P. Snow

Not only survival, but further evolution!
                                        —Jonas Salk

Facts and Values

One of the most common criticisms of Sperry's work—especially by philosophers—involves his conviction that facts and values are not in principle separated.

Decades of debate can be summarized this way: "The fact that something *is* cannot therefore imply that it *ought* to be. The first is a statement about a fact; the second is a value judgment. Each of these statements belongs in a fundamentally different category—in a different world of thinking." Unfortunately, a detailed discussion of these arguments would be of little help to us, because nearly all of the participants have been philosophers with little or no interest in the relevance of the theory of evolution to the question.

Evolutionary theory puts values in a new light. An organism possessing foresight and imagination needs guidelines to choose among different possible avenues of action. Values provide such guidelines. Choices in the right direction lead to survival and the retention of the chosen values in the brains and cultures of the living.

In that case, then, are we justified in joining Alexander Pope in declaring "whatever is, is right"? To a certain extent, yes, but only if we accept the arbitrary judgment that the present world is the best possible one and that superior wisdom could not have achieved better—and only if we ignore the inconvenient fact that the human species, through its one-sided valuation of intelligence and competitiveness, has brought itself to the brink of extinction. A persuasive argument *against* the assumption that because certain values have been involved in our survival so far we will need them for further survival has been brought forth by Roy L. Walford, a medical doctor.

> What is needed to keep alive is not another blueprint out of Adam Smith, Karl Marx, or John Maynard Keynes. Simple reworking and extensions of older economic and political philosophies may not suffice [to solve] the problems of our current evolutionary stage. What we need is a jump or mutational event in the social structure, a discontinuity, an abrupt historical change in man's whole orientation toward himself and his problems.[1]

But to say that facts and values are not in principle distinct is by no means the same as saying that what is, ought to be. On the contrary, those who reject the argument that facts and values belong to "different worlds" demand *critical evaluation* of any line of thinking, openness to new insights, and scrutiny of everything that has always been taken for granted.

Considerations like these lie at the basis of Sperry's insistence that our salvation may depend upon the use of science to obtain social values, and he would certainly identify himself with philosopher Leon Kass's contention that "prejudgments or ideologies" cannot be allowed to supplant genuine thought.[2]

So important is the subject to Sperry that he has incorporated it into all his work on philosophy. For example, he has argued for public support of science not just because of its role in technological advance but because of science's "unmatched potential for the shaping of ethical values."[3] A science-based ethics, Sperry believes, is our best hope for a viable future. He looks forward to the time when science will be "the best source, method, and authority for determining the ultimate criteria of moral value and those ultimate ethical axioms and guideline beliefs to live and govern by."[4]

The traditional fact/value, is/ought distinctions of the philosopher, Sperry believes, simply disappear from the perspective of a neuroscientist. The brain is constantly processing incoming facts—the input of the senses—and comparing them with already existing information on values and ethics. Facts help determine values, and values help determine which facts are considered important.[5]

Needless to say, this point of view has met with considerable resistance. Among the objections: (1) Whether or not established values are involved in brain functions has nothing to do with the question of whether these values are the *right* ones. Value judgments have to be made *independently* of what is. (2) Science might be able to determine subordinate values, but never the "ultimate criteria" of human existence. (3) If values emerge from brain function and therefore, according to Sperry's ideas of downward causation, help determine brain activity, how can we turn around and say that brain activity is involved in determining values? Is that not a circular argument? The determination should occur *only* from the whole to the parts, not in the opposite direction.

The last objection is easiest to counter. As we explained earlier, whole-part interactions consist of intricate, tightly interwoven, cause-effect relationships in every direction. These are not static, but dynamic, especially in the brain, where new constellations are formed every split-second. Though selective attention to downward causation reveals factors of unexpected importance, each whole is first of all the creation of its parts. The qualities, properties, and laws of the parts, together with their relationship to one another, determine the qualities, properties, and laws of the new active whole. This in turn affects a large variety of ongoing activities, including those of the parts that created it.

The laws and properties of the whole may be thoroughly different from those of the parts; at the same time, though, those holistic properties will differ from those of *other* wholes created by *other* parts. As new facts are taken into account, *a new whole is being created;* a new constellation of facts and values takes over the task of the previous one, which has vanished with the demolition of incorrect knowledge. The process does not work, however, if values, even subordinate ones, are thought of as absolute. In that case, new and improved knowledge is demolished, instead of the old and incorrect, in order to preserve established values. In short, we would maintain an ideology in the face of overwhelming, contradictory evidence. All of Sperry's arguments, and their urgency, are motivated by his insight that the fate of mankind and of our earth hinges on the acceptance of new factual knowledge.

What we said here also answers, at least in part, the first objection we considered. But we must distinguish between ultimate and subordinate values. *All* values pertain to humanity's ultimate aim to survive as a species. (This is generally agreed upon as quite an acceptable aspiration, except by some extraordinarily devout dualists.) Interpretations of *how* that aim is to be achieved, however, differ widely, depending upon what facts are available. Those facts *must* be accurate if the main goal is to be reached, and the nature of those facts will shape the character of subordinate values helping us to reach that ultimate aim.

One might argue that some methods of survival are so reprehensible that they would turn us into animals. True enough; but in that case we would not survive as a species; our species is the *human* one with all the qualities cherished by human beings, including aspirations toward something higher, something beyond ourselves, something of the divine.

As to the second objection, in the end one can only agree. Yes, ultimate value criteria lie outside the realm of science. There is no way to prove *objectively* (without invoking our feelings and emotions, our subjective experience) that the fate of mankind is a worthwhile concern. Even Jacques Monod, after thoroughly discussing the issue with various philosophers, agreed that his own ultimate goal, the striving for objective knowledge, could not be derived from science but must be accepted as an axiom. For Sperry, it is clear that "ultimate values" cannot be derived from science; acceptance of the Grand Design of Nature as intrinsically good must be taken as axiomatic, as something *self-evident.*

It might be expected that "reverence for the Grand Design of Nature" would demand a hands-off policy, an imperative *not* to interfere with nature, under the assumption that "whatever is, is right." Instead, arguments *against* "whatever is, is right" (as, for instance the one above by Walford) show a far better understanding of the process of evolution, which, in fact, embodies the command to constantly replace "what is" with something better.

When scientist Max Delbruck declares that the future course of history will *not* be decided by further discoveries in science but by questions in human values, and when Jonas Salk recommends exposing men's minds to the laws of nature to instill the wisdom necessary to replace our damaging reliance on physical power,[6] both are speaking of the same process—a replacement of "what is" with something better. What we have is neither a prescription for complacency nor an acquiescence in the status quo, but a challenge to do better.

Unfortunately, unlike Delbruck, Salk, or Sperry, the average scientist has found it hard to overcome his traditional materialist-reductionist viewpoint—the imperative to distance himself from any value-judgment whatsoever. This perspective, which has filtered from science into the rest of our society (and brought about a backlash of religious fundamentalism), is leading to an unsatisfactory situation which is arousing widespread concern. Sir Ernst Gombrich, for instance, entitled his bicentennial address to the American Academy of Arts and Sciences in 1982 "Focus on the Arts and Humanities" and said:

> I want to suggest that we should restore to the humanities the sense of wonder, or admiration, and also of horror, in other words, a sense of value. That stance of non-involvement, the attitude of "nil admirari" which is too often adopted in the name of scientific detachment seems to me to upset that balance between objectivity and subjectivity which I consider essential.[7]

The same kind of concern moved Sperry to erect an entire system of ethics based upon the close relationship between science and values. He began with one axiom:

> The Grand Design of Nature perceived broadly in four dimensions, including the forces that move the universe and created man, with special focus on evolution in our own biosphere, is something intrinsically good that it is right to preserve and enhance, and wrong to destroy or degrade.[8]

As long as we make sure that that axiom is phrased in a way that is scientifically valid—that all its terms are open to the usual scientific scrutiny, questioning, and definition—then we can build up an entire system of belief on this foundation. The list of axioms can be expanded, taking care to make sure the whole system remains self-consistent. Faced with the need to make judgments about certain values or morals, we can turn back to the fundamental axioms, using them as final arbitrators. Of course, Sperry adds, just as with the American Constitution or British common law or any other set of precepts, rules, or laws, there will be debates over how the axioms should be interpreted.[9] But because the axioms are finally rooted in a scientific view of the universe, scientific methods can be employed to resolve such debates.

An axiom is chosen because everyone agrees it is self-evident. In Sperry's view, the methods that nature uses to create cannot be questioned, and therefore they must be accepted as universally valid ethical principles. How to practically apply those principles may then be discussed later.

Since Monod starts with a different axiom, making the striving for objective knowledge man's highest goal, and Christianity would add faith in revelation as transmitted through the Bible as yet another axiom, we are faced with a choice among axioms.

We are convinced that serious and thorough study considering the consequences of accepting any one of these three axioms would arrive at the choice of Sperry's Grand Design if, but *only* if, the forward thrust of evolution is interpreted in the sense Salk sees it: as the search for compatible creative relationships to bring about a new whole, a new, powerful, and influential body of wisdom to take the place of present mutually destructive schemes. Any other interpretation—for instance, the social Darwinism of Herbert Spencer or the individualism-run-rampant of Ayn Rand—would turn Sperry's axiom into a nightmare for mankind and lead to the extinction of humanity.

Many critics of Sperry's fact-versus-value stand are, however, not only concerned with the choice of an ultimate frame of reference; they doubt that such a framework could be useful in arriving at specific day-to-day decisions. For example, one reviewer writes:

> Even if all the world were to recognize with Mr. Sperry the self-evident goodness of such things as the preservation of the environment, the elimination of poverty, the reduction of overpopulation and the abolition of nuclear arms, science alone could not dictate how to achieve those ends. Is the damage to the environment caused by stripmining justified if it makes the United States less dependent on Middle Eastern oil? If it is worth $135 million to forestall an epidemic that might claim a million lives, how much is it worth to save only 10 lives?[10]

Sperry's reply is that the global ethic to which science leads will do as well as any moral code; and he agrees that evolving nature itself is full of contradictions, and that it can provide us only with an approximate sense of direction if viewed from a larger perspective. But this sense of direction, he is convinced, is better than anything else we have.

However, along with the criticism, there have appeared, with increasing frequency, expressions of support and understanding, sometimes so complete that they seem like echoes of the thoughts and perspectives Sperry tries to transmit.

Among those who fully grasped the necessity to insist on the tenet that facts and values are interrelated was Dr. M. E. Grenander, who ended her review of *Science and Moral Priority* by concluding that the urgency and power of Sperry's views lies in his farsighted approach to values and "his nightmare vision of a world ending not with a bang but with the whimper of starving billions on a famished and exhausted planet."[11]

Focus on the Mind-Brain Problem

The criticisms considered so far involve both Sperry's mind-brain theory and his views on values. In the following, we will concentrate on three main objections to his solution of the mind-brain problem.

1. Panpsychism explains consciousness better than any other theory.
2. A nonmaterial entity cannot possibly influence a material one.
3. Sperry's concept of materialism is outdated.

As for the first—that panpsychism is superior, as an explanation of consciousness, to Sperry's theory—we should start by explaining that panpsychism is the belief that a little bit of consciousness, or preconsciousness, is contained even in subatomic particles. Every new unit of organization combines these preexisting parts of consciousness into more potent entities. An atom is more conscious than a subatomic particle, a molecule more than an atom, a cell more than a molecule; and rocks, plants, and animals all have their own more or less evolved degrees of consciousness. Man, of course, possesses consciousness of the highest degree.

Such a perception of nature stands in complete contrast to that based on the concept of emergence, with its understanding that the forces of nature, interacting with one another in unprecedented ways, may bring about completely unexpected phenomena, properties, and laws, and that consciousness is but one of billions over billions of potential new creations, most of which may never come into being. The difficulties inherent in panpsychism are obvious. *If* a small element of consciousness exists in subatomic particles, why not also a small element of all those other billions of possibilities? John Eccles once declared that to accept panpsychism means to accept the belief that nothing new can ever be created by nature.

Arthur Peacocke, an English professor of chemistry, an ordained minister, and another person who has attempted to bridge the science-religion chasm,[12] has noted that the belief that some spark of consciousness resides in everything—right down to atoms and their components—is simply an "inadequate model" of reality. It would be equally incorrect to hold that, since the compound water is wet, individual molecules of hydrogen and oxygen are also, *in themselves,* possessed of "inherent wetness." In any case, the concept of emergence offers a much more palatable explanation of consciousness. In Peacocke's own words, "That mental activities are genuinely emerging and are not theoretically, or conceptually, or linguistically, reducible to neurophysiological events renders unnecessary, it seems to me, such a panpsychic model for preserving an emphasis on the mental potentialities of matter."[13]

Many scientists have raised another objection to Sperry's theory of emergent causation: a nonmaterial entity, they say, cannot possibly influence a material one. (This objection, we should note, is restricted to the world of science. In most religions, of course, the idea of consciousness as causal finds ready acceptance—but its counterpart, the concept of the mind as emergent from brain-function, is consistently rejected in favor of a dualistic view.)

Many supporters of Sperry's philosophy have countered this argument by noting that, for Sperry, mental events are actually an aspect of matter *if* matter is but correctly understood.[14] Approaching the issue from a different direction, Edmond M. Dewan has pointed out that even in a field as far removed from brain science as engineering, entities with no physical existence can emerge and act as "virtual governors" of physical processes. We shall consider his ideas in detail later; suffice it to say for now that good arguments can be made that nonmaterial emergent properties, such as mind, can affect matter.

The third criticism to consider—that Sperry's concept of materialism is outdated—is perhaps the most substantial. There is evidence that the hard-edged materialism of the 1950s and '60s has softened, and that as far as neuroscience is concerned most materialists are willing to take a less doctrinaire stand. William Uttal, the author of a textbook with a strong materialist and reductionist slant, *The Psychobiology of Mind,* writes that "the organizational pattern of the parts rather than the nature of the parts . . . is probably the correct level of inquiry with regard to the specific subject-matter of the mind-brain problem."[15] Such a concession does not satisfy Sperry, who still rejects materialism and reductionism on the grounds that they are concerned solely with isolated parts and part-properties. Instead, he suggests that an entity be thought of not simply as "a system of just material components" but as "a combined space-time-mass-energy manifold. Think of space [he argues] being bent around and molded by the material parts and time as similarly being defined by events in temporal and moving systems." To reduce such a system to merely its material elements is a gross oversimplification. The "space-time-components" of the system, "interfused with, shaped by, and demarcated by the material components," are crucial in creating the properties of the entity; and scientific laws describing the material elements of the system do not encompass the space-time components: "At-

tempts to recognize them in so-called 'collective' and 'cooperative' effects tend to fall short of an adequate recognition of the
basic importance of the space-time elements.''[16]

Still, the question persists: Why does Sperry treat the matter
as if materialists actually have not mended their ways? There
are two factors to consider.

First, most materialists pay only lip service to holistic properties. Their conceptions of reality are constructed strictly from
parts belonging to the microworld of their respective fields.
Molecular biologists, like Monod, believe that the world can
comfortably be explained in terms of molecules. Quantum physicists see reality in terms of dancing subatomic particles. Although they may refer offhandedly to the existence of larger
wholes, these do not actually count for much in the final analysis. At heart the materialists remain convinced that the whole *is*
the sum of its parts. It is this internal, emotional, subjective,
private world of the materialists that is so influential in mold-
ing our society's conceptions of reality. To that world Sperry
addresses himself.

The second factor is historical in nature. In the mid-sixties,
when Sperry first confronted the mind-brain problem, the
worldview of the materialists was, even officially, completely
different. Not until the late 1970s, when the worst excesses of
materialism, reductionism, and behaviorism had subsided,
could textbook writers like Uttal point out the importance of
the organization of parts of a larger system, as opposed to the
precise nature of each of those parts. When Sperry started to
campaign against the meaninglessness of the severely oversim-
plified materialistic view of the world, it took considerable
courage. Still struck by the boldness his pioneering views once
possessed, and hoping to emphasize their importance, Sperry
continues to prefer his old arguments against materialism,
counterproductive though they may now be. But, it is fair to
add, these arguments did help to undermine faith in materialism in the first place.

Peacocke, who shares most of Sperry's convictions, gives a

fine example of how contemporary understanding of matter can be taken into account when he separates reductionism from materialism and elevates the latter. Is the idea that mind emerges from brain function "simple old-fashioned material-ism" in another, more sophisticated guise? Peacocke asks. True enough, "no *thing* is there" apart from the building blocks of matter—no vital force beyond scientific explanation, no ani-mating supernatural spirit. But, Peacocke notes, this new kind of materialism "is not 'old-fashioned' if by that one means that this is all there is to be said and the deterministic laws of phys-ics and chemistry describe all." If we are to talk in a compre-hensive way of the properties of matter, then "the mental ca-pabilities of matter" must be included in that listing. As Peacocke remarks, "we did not know of what matter, as de-scribed by physics and chemistry (or even biophysics and bio-chemistry), was capable until brains had evolved." The terms *materialism* and *reductionism* need not be synonymous: our con-cept of matter's properties and capacities can be widened far beyond the "old-fashioned" limits of materialism.[17] The "old-fashioned" concept of matter was perhaps just as premature and uninformed as the "old-fashioned" concept of mind, and both may approach each other as science proceeds.

In addition to these objections, the special nature of causality within the whole-part relationship is occasionally misunder-stood and equated with the linear cause-effect relationship of billiard balls. Within a whole (or a system), cause-effect rela-tionships are multiple, extremely complex, and tightly inter-woven. The work of the philosopher Mario Bunge and other experts in the area supports our view that parts simultaneously *produce* the whole (through their specific constellations among each other) and *are* the whole (because nothing is added to the parts from the outside), and that their specific constellations are determined through properties these parts have *within systems.* The latter position receives especially strong support from the philosopher William Wimsatt, who provides detailed and thor-ough explanations for the difference in the behavior of parts *in isolation* and parts *within systems*. Wimsatt refers specifically to Sperry's mind-brain philosophy[18] and "would seem ultimately to strengthen it greatly."[19] Through his point of view, a large number of heated arguments around the subject are simply rendered baseless. Similarly, Bunge devotes much attention to the special nature of causality within systems and even goes so far as to suggest a separate name for the phenomenon to clearly distinguish it from our more common understanding of causality.[20] Although complex, the topic deals with the very core of the part-whole relationship; we will therefore return to Wimsatt and Bunge later.

Focus on Values

The turmoil caused by Sperry's work on ethics is even more lively and varied than the response to his mind-body theory. Often the same individuals reacted both positively and negatively.

One reviewer of *Science and Moral Priority* regretted that "Sperry neglects to give much weight to our human penchant for totally irrational activity" but believes that "if his book opens the desired dialogue between science, ethics, and religion that results in the worldwide ethical system Sperry foresees, its shortcomings will be amply redeemed."[21]

The inhumaneness of humanitarian antiscience was demonstrated by another reviewer who deplored the fact that we no longer hold the agent responsible if there is a plausible causal account for an action, as, for example, if it can be attributed to schizophrenia or a brain tumor. "What would happen to the idea of responsibility," he complained, "if Sperry's science of values were sufficiently developed to explain in causal terms the values held by everyone?"[22]

In this view, the punishment of innocents (such as persons with brain tumors) is not seen as wrong; instead, its elimination is seen as a deplorable development that must not be continued! Should we reverse it, then, perhaps rolling the clock back to the time when witches were held responsible for hurricanes and burned at the stake if such natural tumults resulted in the sinking of a ship? Burning witches saved no one from hurricanes, but the discovery of the reasons for these natural disasters and the development of warning systems *did*. Should we reject science and insist on the punishment of innocents, or should we try to find reasons for misfortune and learn to protect ourselves against it?

Still another reviewer of Sperry's *Science and Moral Priority* claimed to find correlations between Sperry's views on ethics and Teilhard de Chardin's mysticism. We have already discussed the difference between these two points of view; Teilhard believes in evolution as directed by a higher intellect, striving toward a finite end, and melting mankind through population pressure into one loving community. Sperry believes that evolution is directed through natural selection (that is, the interaction of emergent phenomena), that it is an unending process as long as matter and energy exist, and that increasing population pressure would lead to severe degradation of the quality of life. As the renowned evolutionist George Gaylord Simpson explained, the study of evolution does not reveal the straight-ahead, upward drive one might expect if it were directed by higher beings. Instead, organisms move in to fill each new ecological niche as it is created, after which plants and animals continue to slowly evolve, becoming more and more fitted to their place in nature.

> The fossil record shows very clearly that there is no central line leading steadily, in a goaldirected way, from a protozoan to man. Instead, there has been continual and extremely delicate branching, and, whatever course we follow through the branches, there are repeated changes, both in the rate and direction of evolution.[23]

As eons passed, however, chance activity became more and more directed, not through some outer being or power, nor through any inner power other than that inherent in the mutual influence of evolved phenomena upon one another. Evolution proceeds toward no preset goal; new constellations are constantly tried and discarded, and unless our highest mental capacities, both analytic and intuitive, are fully recognized as legitimate factors in that interplay of natural forces and used wisely, the human experiment, too, may end in failure. Something new will evolve, but whether we would consider it "better," whether it would embody our dreams and hopes, or whether it would seem as alien and empty of purpose as the insects which have flourished, some of them virtually unchanged, for hundreds of millions of years, we cannot know.

Emergent causation has been interpreted as *automatically* leading to increased order and cognition, whether or not humanity perishes in the process. Belief in the independent, autonomous progress of life toward the better brings with it the danger that concern for our species' fate will be neglected and that its accumulated wisdom will be discarded like dust upon the winds of time. We are convinced that if we take the "easy out," if we console ourselves by thinking that if humanity does not achieve maturity and avoid extinction then some other intelligent species will arise that will be kinder, wiser, less receptive to violent solutions, then we seek to evade coresponsibility for the direction evolving nature will take in the future.

Furthermore, the upward thrust of evolution is something that can only be discerned from a distance, and only if the entire process is taken into account. When the focus is narrowed, the phenomenon disappears. Thus, we believe, whether any measure taken to improve our fate will actually turn out to be an improvement or lead to disaster is so difficult to foretell that constant vigilance along the way and constant readiness to change are essential. Ideologies that promote independent thought, yes; ideologies that substitute for it, no.

The one thing shared by Sperry and Teilhard is a deep reverence for the phenomenon of evolution, a reverence that lends sensitivity and power to their language. Because Sperry speaks about nature in words that do not destroy the magic of its impact on those whose minds have not lost the ability to wonder, he has been accused of mysticism. But if it is magic he is able to experience and transmit, it is the magic of an unreduced, undistorted reality.

Sperry's view of an undistorted reality embodies the experience of an ineffable striving for improvement which flows through nonhuman and human nature alike. In part this is the sort of right-hemisphere knowledge which dissolves when pinned down and dissected, yet which is immensely valuable. Sperry's suggestion that our highest values should advance "the trends of the creative process toward improved quality of existence" has led some to accuse him of failing to deal with the problem of determining which factors enhance "the quality of existence." And, they add, it remains unclear why the persons best suited for this task are scientists.

Sperry himself responds to such objections with the calm conviction that everyone has a pretty good idea about the meaning of "the quality of existence," that the progress from amoeba to man is undeniable and convincing, and that some good common-sense terms can be defined into nothingness by too-sophisticated arguments. There is no doubt that science can be helpful in drawing our attention to the consequences of present trends for the quality of life in the future.

It must be admitted that the term is far from precise and allows for many different interpretations; but, then, the same can be said for the aims of other philosophies. It is well known that the life work and goals of persons with the best of intentions have been distorted out of all recognition by some of their followers. To prevent or at least ameliorate such a fate, the vigilance of those who best understand the significance of a philosopher's work is essential.

As far as we interpret it, "to further the quality of existence" gives the command "to love" a deeper meaning—more comprehensive, more farsighted, more responsible.

Reflections

It is always revealing and often surprising how different a thinker's work appears when seen through another's eyes.

Supporters are nearly always those already preoccupied with similar subjects and goals. The most valuable contributions to a new way of thinking, however, come from those approaching the subject matter from a different angle—from those who criticize, who disagree, who clarify. Their discovery of flaws, or points of significance, not visible to the original author, and the subsequent rethinking and reworking of the scheme of thought, often lead to a strengthening of the author's point of view.

Upon reflecting on all that has been written by Sperry's critics, by sifting it again and again to reduce it to manageable proportions, it appears that several quite important points have been left unmentioned. To these belong:

1. The problem of dualism. The term can be understood in two different ways: first, in the traditional Cartesian sense, in which the mind resides in a world of its own in an unembodied state; second, in the sense of mind being an emergent of, but not the same as, physico-chemical activity in the brain. Only in the second sense is Sperry a dualist.

2. The relevance of the insight that subjective values emerge from brain function, a process governed by the laws of nature—which means that values and moral commands incompatible with the laws of nature cannot be valid.[24] If we are to live sanely, values we acquire socially must be compatible with those that are part of our innate biological nature.[25]

3. The inability of nonbiologists to comprehend issues, unless explained in detail, that appear crystal clear to biologists. This, in fact, inspired us to write the present book. Sperry's philosophy, and its value for our future, ought to be understandable to everyone.

Part 3

THE HOPE

Our current difficulties call for more thought, not less, albeit also thought of a somewhat different kind. They beckon us to seek *deeper* knowledge, precisely about the adequacy of what we already know—or think we know—and also about the possible knowability of what we have declared to be unknowable.

—Leon Kass

A great man does not exist to be followed slavishly and may be more honored by divergence than by obedience.

—C. Lloyd Morgan

·8·

Toward Left-Hemisphere Acceptance

It takes an intellect of great audacity even to contemplate the possibility that the world view is wrong and the perception right; and it takes an intellect of the highest order of imaginative power to conceive an alternative world view—that is to propose an explanation of the perception instead of merely explaining it away.
—William T. Jones

On the Part-Whole Relationship

Throughout his papers Sperry treats what he calls "space-time factors" as different from—and unexplainable through—the parts of which a whole is constructed in nature.[1] Since different relationships among the same parts bring about wholes with different properties, Sperry insists that reductionism cannot account for emergent new wholes, unless these space and time factors are specifically included.

> I have repeatedly stressed the important causal role of the non-material space-time, pattern, or form factors and suggested that it is helpful to view any entity as not just a collection of material parts but a mass-energy-space-time manifold built on space-time components as well as of matter.[2]

Of course, what Sperry says is true. But reductionists make the same claim. The major preoccupation of chemists and physicists is, in fact, the search for these so-called space-time factors and their effects. In contrast to Sperry, however, reductionists see these critical space-time factors as properties, either of the parts or of the environment of the parts, but in any case as micro-determined—that is, as determined by the way *the parts themselves* behave under different conditions. Thus, carbon atoms form diamonds under high pressure, a substance so hard that it can cut glass; they form soft, pliable, reproducing living organisms in the presence of DNA, normal atmospheric pressure, and diverse metabolic constituents; they form coal under still different circumstances. All of these transformations may be expressed in the language of either macro- or micro-determinism, depending upon the objective of the conversation. (*Macro-determinism* describes a phenomenon in terms of causality from the top downward, micro-determinism in terms of causality from the bottom upward.) Unless the objective is specifically stated, neither micro- nor macro-determinism is wrong. If the objective is "to get at" reality itself, it is best, as Sperry explains, to visualize different levels of organization within reality and to speak and think in terms of the properties and laws of the appropriate level of discourse, because knowledge of the laws and properties of the parts alone is not enough to understand the emergent whole. In short, it is one thing to understand the space-time relationships among the parts; it is quite another to grasp an emerging new phenomenon in a meaningful way. Holistic properties vanish if the parts that bring them about are scrutinized in isolation—just as the smile on the face of a friend cannot be perceived if the crinkles, creases, and dimples producing it are studied under a microscope. But that has nothing to do with the space-time properties of the parts and their possible explanation through the knowledge of the characteristics of the parts.

The smile, for instance, can still not be perceived as such, *even if all the space-time factors among the skin cells and underlying muscle cells producing the smile are known in detail.* Unless we forget about the cells and look at the face, the smile cannot be seen; and unless we forget about the space-time factors and ask about the *reason* for our friend's happiness, the smile cannot be fully explained. When seen and understood in terms of downward causation, a world of meaning enters events and phenomena which otherwise remain meaningless.

Sperry's philosophy does not stand or fall on the question of whether or not space-time factors among the parts can be explained through the knowledge of the parts. In either case in practice a complete understanding of the entire situation demands knowledge of the higher-level causative factors that produce the specific space-time relationships. The question then becomes one of how far in each direction the tangle of cause-effect chains is to be pursued. In theory, the task is endless.

Nor does Sperry's philosophy stand or fall on the fact that in very simple examples—for example, that of a wheel running downhill—holistic properties *can* be and have been predicted (with the help of computers) from a knowledge of part-properties and laws alone. Some object that the analogy of the wheel is not a good example of emergence: whether we predict the wheel's motion on the basis of the motion of individual particles or by means of holistic calculations, these are still descriptions on only one level—that of mechanics. The real problem, it is said, is whether the appearance of new properties *transcending* their levels can or cannot be predicted. However, even if that example is taken to suggest that emergent properties can be predicted in principle in more complex cases, Sperry's philosophy still stands. Prediction *in principle* is not the problem. The problem, to put it in very simple terms, consists of the complete impossibility of ever being able to predict complex emergents *in practice* through micro-determinism alone, at least not when the number of the multiple causal factors approaches infinity and nothing but our limited nervous system, together with its extension through instruments, is available to attempt the task. The danger of the "prediction-in-principle" worldview lies in hidden "prediction-in-practice" assumptions to which it might lead. The result would be a severely distorted assessment of reality. Clearly, the preceding discussion refers only to phenomena known to us. *Completely* new emergents—

those beyond anything we even *can* imagine—would be unpredictable, even in principle.

Most experts in the field, including Monod, agree that, in general, emergent properties cannot be predicted, whether in practice or in principle, even though they can be explained through micro-events after they have occurred. Though we are able to predict simple holistic emergents and their effects in practice, as in the case of an explosion involving a finite number of well-known factors, we cannot extrapolate that to an argument for predictability in general. At a certain level of complexity the capacities of our nervous system, even when extended by computers, would be overpowered by the sheer number of possibilities and unknowns—even at the level of mechanics. Going beyond that level, these difficulties are compounded. No one could seriously maintain that the appearance of consciousness could have been foretold merely through the knowledge of how complex systems of brain cells interact with one another.

Other intellectuals, including some who are thoroughly acquainted with microbiology, reject even the possibility of tracing back any properties *after* they have emerged, merely through knowledge of the component micro-events. We believe that the difficulty lies in the assumption of a fundamental difference between matter as static and emergence as an unexplainable mystical process. This difference dissolves if the fundamental unity of reality and its dynamic quality are completely understood. With this understanding, emergence, a result of changing relationships, becomes a natural process. The contrast between matter and nonmatter vanishes as it is realized that only in exceptional cases strongly and intimately interacting forces lead to our experience of solids. Nature is not therefore drained of its magic; it is enriched. But the true and real wonder lies in the *origin* of the dynamic process, not only in its later manifestations.

Again, the argument that downward causation is active in our reality system—the key tenet of Sperry's philosophy—is independent of how and whether that phenomenon is predictable or explainable, once the dynamic properties of matter are known. Even if every single relationship among parts could be traced and explained through knowledge of micro-events (both of the parts and their environment), the overall organization of these events remains meaningless and unintelligible unless higher-level causal factors are understood and grasped as properties of wholes.

And so it is that Sperry insists that micro-events alone—events at the physical and chemical level—are not enough to fully explain what goes on in the "real world." Some critics have misconstrued that conviction as meaning that he believes in the supernatural or in forces of nature yet unexplained by science. It is partly because of this that the key concept of downward causation is also frequently rejected as unscientific.

The philosopher of science Robert L. Klee, for instance, has said that some concepts of emergence are compatible with micro-determinism, that is, with the view that emergence can be fully explained by the knowledge of parts and their properties. The type of emergence Sperry proposes, involving downward causation, is not one of them. According to Klee, it is "scientifically weak" and therefore to be rejected.[3]

Both Klee and Sperry have presented their arguments in scientific journals. An unnamed referee for one journal states the problem as follows:

> Perhaps the fundamental confusion—or, if not confusion then at least highly questionable premise—is the idea that if micro-determinism prevails then there is simply no room for higher causation to operate. Micro-determinism entails no such thing; for it is entirely possible that higher-level causation operates via underlying micro-causation, rather than being excluded by it.[4]

Yet Sperry would not be satisfied with that solution. He believes that, as soon as a higher level of organization is reached, the new properties "take over and determine the fate of the parts that produced them." That is certainly true; however, the question to be resolved, we believe, is in which situation that knowledge is relevant and in which it is not. During research at the micro-level, for instance, macro-determination may be perceived and interpreted as environmental micro-determination without in any way affecting the result of the research. Consider, for instance, the effect of stomach acid upon the lining of the stomach, which may be investigated independently of the knowledge of the causes of stomach ulcers. A doctor dealing with a patient, however, depends upon a more holistic conception of the disease if he is to be helpful.

Sperry insists strenuously upon the principle of downward causation precisely because it has been deplorably neglected where it is most urgently needed: in interhuman relations. He emphasizes and overemphasizes the importance of emergence, of holistic concepts, and of downward causation—preferring to invite misunderstanding rather than to lessen the impact of what he has to say.

In 1983, for instance, he went so far as to reintroduce the concept of *vitalism* as best describing emerging properties of living organisms—ignoring the shudders of his scientific friends. The word *vitalism* had been earlier attached to the notion that living things are animated by a special force, different from those active in the inorganic world, and it had been eliminated from science early in this century because of its mystical connotations. Nevertheless, Sperry refuses to use an alternative. "A new word would be better," he says, "but in this case I'm not sure whether we should revise the language just because a good word has mistakenly been given bad associations."[5]

Then he explains:

> We biologists had merely been searching in the wrong places. You don't look for vital forces among atoms and molecules. You look among living things—among cells and animals responding to each other, reproducing, breathing, eating, running, flying, swimming, building nests, and so on.
>
> The special vital forces that distinguish living things from non-

living things are emergent, holistic properties, not properties of their physico-chemical components. Nor can they be fully explained in mechanistic terms. This doesn't mean that they are in any way supernatural or mystical. Those who conceived of vital forces in supernatural terms were just as wrong as those who denied the existence of these forces.[6]

Were it not for the sentence "Nor can they be fully explained in mechanistic terms," scientists would be delighted. There is no mysticism. Everything falls into place, simply and naturally, and a magnificent vista of reality from a perspective beyond reductionism becomes apparent. But why should Sperry think that his vital forces cannot be explained through physics and chemistry? Could he covertly believe in supernatural forces or powers after all? Such sentences can easily be misunderstood and lead to the rejection of his entire philosophy by scientists unless they are read very carefully, and unless we grasp that he merely means that the properties of wholes cannot be explained or described in words that describe the properties of the parts, because parts in isolation do not *have* any holistic properties. A single water molecule, for instance, cannot freeze. Water freezes when the temperature drops to the point where a great many molecules spontaneously arrange themselves into a crystal lattice. Of course, it must be kept in mind that "parts in isolation" exist only in the abstract. Each part is at the same time a whole with respect to parts at the next lower level—and these again are wholes for parts at a level still lower, and so on.

Such an image of reality does not cease at the level of individual consciousness. Each individual is part of humankind, and humankind, in turn, is part of our ecosystem. This is where the theory of emergent causation connects to ethics. Many critics of Sperry's philosophy are unable to see this connection; but as we feel ourselves part of nature, which we are, we ought more willingly, and as a matter of course, accept nature's—our creator's—higher-order directives. Our life and health and that of our biosphere depend upon a delicate balance.

Sperry's search for a more valid conception of reality is suggesting an answer to the question "What makes life worth living?"—an answer that combines humanity's need to strive for higher goals with its need to strive for logical consistency.

In addition to strongly emphasizing holistic phenomena, however, Sperry has intermittently, and especially lately, made efforts to integrate his theory of emergent causation with the latest research in modern physics. Recently, after discussions with a number of young physicists, he admitted that it does not matter whether or not space-time relationships among parts producing new wholes are explainable through the properties of the parts (and those of the environment), or even whether in simple cases holisitc properties can be predicted through the characteristics of their parts. What counts is that such *new emergents occur, and that they become new causative forces in the universe.* In making that concession, Sperry has removed the main barrier against the acceptance of his philosophy in the world of traditional science, he has strengthened the fundaments of his philosophy, and he has made his ideas accessible to a major part of the population that would otherwise reject them.

Moreover, he has eliminated the need to wrestle with unresolvable paradoxes, something that still weighs on the mind of many conscientious persons. The Klee-Sperry referee, for instance, after having struggled with these paradoxes for over twenty years, says that consciousness "is mysterious and gives us the feeling that we have the power to control certain events, and there is a sense in which we do. Yet, the logical issues are also clear and have a power of their own."

To convey his inner tension, the referee cites a Victorian poem, "Dover Beach" by Matthew Arnold, which expresses the pain of the clash between humanism and science.

> . . . for the world, which seems
> To lie before us like a land of dreams,
> So various, so beautiful, so new,
> Hath really neither joy nor love nor light,

Nor certitude, nor peace, or help for pain;
And we are here as on a darkling plain
Swept with confused alarms of struggle and flight
Where ignorant armies clash at night.

With the word *really,* Arnold leads the reader into the world of traditional science from which subjective experience is excluded. With the reinstatement of consciousness into our worldview through his philosophy of emergent causation, Sperry permits us to recognize that our world is not only more beautiful but also more "real" than that of materialistic and reductionistic science. The "real" world is not one from which human beings are excluded; they and their inner lives are part of it. There really is joy and love and light in the world.

The battle for left-hemisphere acceptance is not one that Sperry will win alone. As Darwin has his "bulldog"—Thomas Huxley—so, too, has Sperry his supporters and defenders. Let us consider six of them and their ideas.[7]

Dewan and the Virtual Governor

Edmond M. Dewan, at home in the rigorous discipline of control system engineering, contrasts the great physicist Paul A. M. Dirac's statement that "God is a mathematician" with his own conviction that "God is the ultimate engineer (control, information, chemical, electrical, mechanical, . . .)."[8] He is fascinated by the inventions of nature, sometimes millions of years old, which are most often discovered only *after* human beings have reinvented them. Why are men blind to such phenomena before? Dewan's resolution to walk through the world with open eyes led him to understand, accept, and defend Sperry's theory of emergent causation as soon as he encountered it.

Earlier, we touched on the question of whether nonmaterial emergent properties can affect material objects and systems. This is not a problem unique to neuroscience. Drawing on his own background in engineering technology, Dewan provides examples of emergent properties which have no physical existence, but which nevertheless influence physical entities causally. These properties supervene on the activity of individual technical units in the same way that consciousness supervenes on brain events.[9]

The simplest of these examples is the *virtual governor,* which emerges when individual electric power generators are linked in a national electric power grid. Isolated generators, set for the same speed, will vary considerably after some time. Interconnected, however, they "beat as one" through the transfer of excess energy from the faster ones to the slower ones. The term *virtual governor,* coined in 1961 by Norbert Wiener and now in common use for that phenomenon, describes a regulator that is not found in a single location, but which is found throughout the *whole.* Noting that "man often seems to reinvent principles of communciation and control which were already found long ago by Nature," Dewan points out that the virtual governor emerges from a system of electric generators in a way analogous to the emergence of mind from matter.

Virtual governors emerge in other systems as well. The phenomenon was first observed three hundred years ago by the great scientist Christian Huygens, the inventor of the pendulum clock, who noticed it when he observed that two of his pendulum clocks eventually came to tick in unison. Huygens also succeeded in finding its cause: the movement of the two clocks' common support.

The best known example of synchronized oscillation in biology is the pumping movement of the heart muscle cells. No biology student who has observed heart development under the microscope will ever forget seeing the single and irregularly twitching heart muscle cells in a developing egg begin to synchronize their movements and convert their varying twitches into a unified and exquisitely calibrated heartbeat.

A virtual governor does not physically exist; rather it is, in Dewan's words, "an emergent property of the entire system which goes far beyond what any single unit can accomplish in accuracy and power . . . and which supervenes in the behavior of the individual units." Dewan's comparison of a description of the virtual governor with Sperry's 1969 paper on consciousness as an emergent property is striking. They can be interpreted and understood as phenomena of a similar nature, though having vastly different degrees of complexity.

From the description of the simple virtual governor, Dewan proceeds to the concept of *generalized mutual entrainment,* which embodies more sophisticated control systems from *optimal control* and *adaptive control* to *generalized optimal superadaptive control.* Like the virtual governor, all these more intricate devices were also invented by nature, long before man discovered them.

Optimal control consists of the joining of different feedback control factors into one. For instance, information on speed, drag, thrust, altitude, and so forth is needed to arrive at the trajectory and parameter settings that will minimize the fuel consumption of an airplane. The problem of finding these optimal settings is solved with the help of a mathematical function, the *performance index.* Nature uses survivability as its performance index.

The interaction of a number of optimal control systems leads to the emergence of a superoptimal control system, a system in which performance indexes for different tasks lead to one superperformance index for the whole.

Still more remarkable is the use of adaptive control. Feedback itself is a means of adapting; but ordinary feedback is often insufficient. An aircraft, for instance, flying from a lower altitude into a higher one with less air pressure will finally have to be controlled with small rockets instead of gliding on air. Both methods are used at intermediate heights. In short, the method of coping depends upon the altitude; or, more generally, adaptation to a different environment becomes necessary. Both human engineers and nature have developed automatic devices capable of such adaptation. Dewan explains:

> The idea of adaptive control can be generalized. Consider superadaptive control. In this case one could have a feedback device

modify a feedback device which modifies the main feedback control. In other words, one could have a device which modifies its *method* by which it modifies its method of control. This would indeed increase adaptive capability. Furthermore, one can imagine any number of levels of superadaptability; thus, there is in principle no apparent limit to how far one could generalize in this dimension! (No one knows at this time the degree to which Nature has seen fit to go, but no doubt she's gone further than we have.)[10]

An inconspicuous footnote on the same page refers to an aircraft with a sophisticated control system that changed into a system of self-destruction when the aircraft entered denser air oriented in an unanticipated way. According to Dewan, it is typical for supersophisticated complexes to turn into self-destructive systems on encountering unanticipated circumstances!—Food for thought.

Discussing the reality of a nonphysical *governor,* Dewan points out that each theory has its own "level of reality." Temperature, pressure, and heat are all considered "real" in the context of thermodynamics, while they are understood as the product of the random motions of huge numbers of atoms or molecules in the context of statistical mechanics. Thus, from the perspective of statistical mechanics, thermodynamics is a *phenomenological theory.* It follows that qualities that are illusions from the point of view of statistical mechanics are realities from the point of view of thermodynamics.

According to Dewan, causal consciousness in Sperry's sense arises out of the tremendous number of ongoing interactions in the brain, which involve (in his words) "large numbers of superadaptive optimum control systems arranged into a hierarchical mutually cooperative structure—of sublime and majestic engineering dimensions!"[11]

Using the language of the practical scientist and examples from the empirical world, Dewan makes emergent causation palatable to a sector of the population that might otherwise remain untouched.

Wimsatt and Levels of Organization

The work of philosopher William Wimsatt provides a sharp contrast to engineer Dewan's practical, concrete, and compact development of Sperry's ideas. Wimsatt's contribution to the debate is highly abstract and complex. This is hardly surprising, since it addresses a completely different sector of our society: philosophers of science with a strongly analytical and academic bent. Marked by painstaking thoroughness, Wimsatt's major paper of the topic clarifies, from the philosophical point of view, several issues in Sperry's theory which otherwise could be the subject of damaging criticism.[12] These include the difference between the properties of parts in isolation and the properties of parts within wholes and the difference between context-dependent and context-independent reduction. (It is typical of Wimsatt's meticulous way of thinking that the publication of the proceedings of a symposium on questions of consciousness and the brain—dealing largely with Sperry's work and thought—had to be delayed *three years* while he reworked and revised the paper he had already read at the 1973 meeting.)

The philosophical question Wimsatt tried to answer is deceptively simple: Is it possible to claim that the whole is different from its parts and at the same time explain the whole through its parts? He believes that such a feat is possible if we use a new analysis of reductionism from a "functional dynamic perspective" (to be explained below) that he has developed, and that provides a much different view of reductionism than the one usually accepted. Also essential is a thorough understanding of the relationship of different levels of organization to one another.

Concerning the properties of the parts, Wimsatt differentiates between *relational properties,* which only exist within a configuration, and properties of isolated parts. Relational properties emerge only through specific relationships among parts within a system, and can rarely be precisely located. These are the properties which, according to Sperry, are overlooked by reductionists. By distinguishing between these two kinds of properties, Wimsatt throws light on Sperry's insistence that emergent wholes can be only partially, not entirely, explained by the properties of the constituents. By "properties of the constituents," Sperry means the properties that constituents have in isolation.

All of Wimsatt's arguments concerning the issue condense to solid philosophical support for the contention that the *specificity* of the space-time relationships of the parts within the whole is crucial—a position that Sperry has advocated vigorously since the beginning of his work in the area. In 1952, Sperry argued that not the nature of the nerve impulses themselves but their patterning was decisive for the occurrence of consciousness.[13] In 1964, he explained consciousness through "cerebral configurations" and "certain specialized cerebral circuits in action."[14] In 1970 he said that "a complete objective description that included the spatial and temporal features of the neural activity, as such, would perforce include the mental properties."[15] So, from early on in his research Sperry understood and described in terms of the relation between brain activity and consciousness the principles that Wimsatt takes great efforts to present in a more general sense. What Wimsatt has done is to frame these concepts in the language of the philosophy of science to attract the attention of such philosophers to the insights of Sperry's theory.

The main portion of Wimsatt's work is dedicated to defining and describing different levels of organization and to examining the problem of *interlevel reduction*. This is the reduction of higher-level entities to lower-level parts, and it is the kind involved in Sperry's mind-brain theory, in contrast to simple one-to-one reduction between entities on the same level of organization. Consider the analogy of the translation of a word from one language into another one. Such translation depends upon the context in which a word is used. Thus, word-for-word translation may produce nonsense, while the expression of an idea in another language is possible if different words are used in different contexts. (Proverbs are prime examples.) Interlevel reduction is similarly dependent on context. Simple one-to-one translation from one organizational level to another might produce a distorted description of reality, but context-dependent translations of larger related entities are nevertheless realistically possible. That is the core idea of Wimsatt's "functional dynamic perspective" on reductionism.

To overcome the difficulties of interlevel reduction in practice, Wimsatt suggests using a procedure he calls *identification*. Through a series of approximations, a closer and closer fit of two theories at two different organizational levels would ensue. At the outset, we would have two different perspectives which explain the same phenomenon. We would slowly adjust these perspectives, first one, then the other, until an identical middle position is reached. Identification does not try to reduce the upper level to the lower one, nor does it advocate a preoccupation with the upper level at the expense of the lower. Instead, both the upper-level perspective and lower-level perspective contribute to the achievement of a realistic middle position.

Sperry did, in fact, use a very similar procedure to arrive at his middle position between materialism and dualism as the most realistic and fruitful description of reality. More often, however, Wimsatt explains, such middle positions are achieved by two warring schools of thought through mutual criticism and the search for proof of each side's convictions. Each victory won by one school of thought leads the opposing one to ameliorate its position somewhat.

An excellent example is the fight, raging during the second half of the last century, between the pioneer of bacteriology, Nobel laureate Robert Koch, and the medical authority Rudolf Virchow. At its height the battle involved almost every medical institute on all continents. The two sides approached the problem from much different perspectives. Koch and his disciples remained glued to the microscope and discovered bacterial causes of disease after disease. Virchow, on the other hand, was convinced that diseases were caused by poverty and neglect. He had cleaned up the slums of Berlin and transformed the city from one of the dirtiest in the world into one of the cleanest in only two decades. Pointing to the drastic reduction in illness his measures had produced, he rejected Koch's evidence. So deeply ingrained was his conviction that *either* bacteria alone *or* poverty alone was the cause of disease that he—the man considered the world's leader in his field, the man for whom an entire institute had been built in the city of Berlin—forbade the study of bacteriology in his institute. He approached the problem from a different level, one in which bacteria had no place. So adamant was his conviction that he still refused to change his mind even when bacteriology became an accepted course in all major medical institutes. Finally, confronted with the choice of either permitting courses on bacteriology or resigning, Virchow resigned.

At some point someone asked the question: Under which conditions do bacteria thrive best? That question led to a step-by-step approach toward a superior middle position: poverty and neglect cause diseases *because* bacteria proliferate in unsanitary slum conditions, and because poverty and neglect lower resistance against them. Today, it is hard to understand how such a self-evident solution could have been missed at the outset, and how the contrast of viewpoints could have led to such violent fights.

We should therefore keep in mind that even today many self-evident solutions for contrasting positions exist to which we are blind—not only in the field of science (where they are most easily found) but also in other fields, most importantly in the areas of politics and religion.

To apply the process Wimsatt calls identification *within* science is not uncommon; to apply it within other fields is much more difficult; but to arrive at a successful middle position between such disparate fields as science and values, as Sperry has done, is extremely rare. Nearly as rare is the capability and willingness to present pioneer ideas in a language that makes them acceptable to new and different circles. Wimsatt has made an exceptional effort to achieve that task, and he has succeeded. As the commentator on Wimsatt's paper in the symposium's final report remarked, Wimsatt "sharpens Sperry's position and would seem ultimately to strengthen it greatly."

Natsoulas and Concern with Criticism

"Our ignorance about brain-function is no argument against an ability we so often put to use." So declared Dr. Thomas Natsoulas, professor of psychology at the University of California at Davis, in a 1984 paper which clearly demonstrated his alignment with Sperry's convictions.[16] Natsoulas is motivated by the theme that brain function cannot be fully explained unless the phenomenon of consciousness is included. Stimulated by the discovery of the same conviction in Sperry's work, he set out to defend Sperry's mind-brain theory in the language of science and from a scientific perspective.

Like Professor Charles Ripley (whose contributions will be discussed shortly), Natsoulas concentrated on those aspects of Sperry's work that are most compatible with traditional, materialistic points of view in neuroscience, while taking care to enlarge and to elevate the outdated concept of the *material*.[17]

In Natsoulas's view, consciousness is ultimately functional. Human beings developed consciousness because they needed to respond to their environment. If an organism doesn't bother to respond to its environment, or if it has no choice as to the nature of that response—regardless of how many "stimuli" are raining upon it from the outside world—then it is not conscious. So we can say that consciousness is *response-dependent*. To make up its mind about what course of action to choose, an organism must take in, make sense of, organize, interpret, join together, and finally remember almost endless numbers of incoming stimuli. Some of this information may not be recalled in order to make a decision for years; some of it may never be. As a result, though consciousness remains primarily response-oriented, even in organisms like human beings which are evolutionarily advanced, it has taken on another dimension, too: "information management," if you like—dealing with stimuli, sorting them, interpreting them, relating them to one another, so that they can be used to respond more effectively to the outside world.

His acceptance of Sperry's worldview led Natsoulas to consider and, in effect, to battle with, seven major objections to Sperry's theories that various critics had raised. Let us work our way through them, one by one, as Natsoulas has dealt with them in his paper.

1. "Objection: [It is] completely unclear how conscious emergent properties 'direct' individual nerve impulses." At the heart of this objection is the question of how the concept of downward causation "cashes out" in the real world. How do seemingly elusive, "fuzzy" emergent properties like thought affect the physical workings of the brain?

Natsoulas's reply: There are already-established—you might call them "hard-wired"—neural patterns, or "circuits," in the brain which give rise to "brain processes," or brain activity. Some of these processes, or, as Natsoulas also terms them, "dynamic pattern properties," will be mental in nature; some won't. The crucial thing to remember is that these pattern properties, though they *emerge from* brain function, are still very much tied to brain function. Brain function affects them and they affect it. Thus it is easy to see the connection between conscious emergent properties—thought—and individual nerve impulses. As Natsoulas summarizes: "Mental properties can affect particular impulses because mental properties belong to the organized neural context in which the impulses occur."

2. "Objection: [In Sperry's view,] consciousness [is] not part of the physical universe."

Natsoulas's reply: Some critics have charged Sperry with conceiving of the mind as *extraphysical* in the same way that Eccles, a convinced dualist, describes it. The charge is wrong: Sperry's papers clearly show that he considers the mind to be "inseparable from the brain process and its structural constraints."

In fact, for Sperry there is nothing "supernatural" or "disembodied" about the nature of thought: though " 'holistic, configurational, gestalt, encompassing, and entitative,' [mental properties] are *nothing more (or less) than or different from* 'dynamic . . . properties of the cerebral circuitry in action.' "[18] Or, simply: mental properties are special. But they are still products of the physical workings of the brain.

3. "Objection: Action of brain processes on brain processes without [the] intervention of alterations in [the] physical environment" is impossible unless viewed in traditional dualist terms.

Natsoulas's reply: Is Sperry a closet dualist? No. Although Sperry emphasizes the importance of mental events, he does not totally ignore twentieth-century psychology's findings about how organisms respond to stimuli presented to them by the environment. Indeed, mental events are part of a continuing response to the outside world. Emerging from brain activity, they are highly sophisticated means of responding to a variety of stimuli.

4. "Objection: No hypothesis about neural mechanisms" is present in Sperry's theory.

Natsoulas's response: Sperry himself has admitted that neuroscience has a long way to go in describing the differences between complex brain activity that produces consciousness and brain activity that does not. Nonetheless, Sperry's theory at least provides us with a good start. To bolster his case, Natsoulas cites Walter B. Weimer who has argued that "only one hypothesis on the nature of consciousness exists in the psychological literature that deserves to be called 'theoretical' " — Sperry's. Competing efforts have been no more than "paraphrastic."[19]

5. "Objection: Why could not brains have evolved exactly as they did without any conscious experience?"

Natsoulas's reply: This issue was broached by a critic who decided that Sperry was merely "a more sophisticated psychoneural identity theorist." (*Psychoneural identity,* to refresh the memory, is the theory that the mind is identical with brain activity and that, therefore, a description of brain activity *alone* would be a sufficient explanation of what goes on in the brain. As a result, mental processes are irrelevant.) But Sperry, unlike psychoneural identity theorists, rejects the notion that the way the brain functions can be adequately described without referring to mental activity.[20] Natsoulas adds:

> The truly complete physical description of the brain must include reference to all mental phenomena, which literally *are* brain-occurrences. Therefore, the brains of higher animals could not have evolved exactly as they have without certain of their processes being mental phenomena, because this would mean that the brains had not evolved exactly as they have. . . . They would be different brains. You just could not have the brains that we have, intact, connected, in good working condition, without also having mental phenomena.[21]

6. "Objection: Emergent subjective properties do not exist." Natsoulas's reply: Critics arguing this point are interpreting language in a way that is too limiting. The instance he gives is the color yellow. What do we mean when we say something is "yellow"? Are we referring only to something that reflects or radiates light of a particular wavelength? Or are we referring to the quality we perceive, in our minds, as "yellowness"? Those who argue that there are no such things as emergent subjective properties take the first stand: they limit the definition of yellow to a purely physical one. But, says Natsoulas, that definition is too narrow: "[certain] words serve to characterize objects in the environment *and* to identify the properties of the perceptual experience that the objects normally produce." He goes on to ask: "Is there serious doubt, really, that yellowness is somehow present to us when we hallucinate a flash of yellow light?" Of course not. Yellowness exists as an aspect of the outside world, yes, but also as a certain sort of inner experience; as an emergent subjective property.

7. "Objection: No satisfactory explanation of how qualities

of sensation relate to their operational effects" is included in Sperry's theory.

Natsoulas's reply: Natsoulas sets himself the task of discovering whether this argument—brought to bear *by Sperry himself* against his original position, as first put forward in 1952—is still valid when applied to his later interpretation of the relationship between mind and brain. His answer: though a complete explanation is not yet in place, "the original weakness may be somewhat less severe because the later writings have been suggesting in a general way the level at which the intrinsic [that is, mental] properties are to be found." In short: we don't yet have a complete theory of how mental properties relate to the workings of specific networks of neurons. But we are slowly working toward one; and as yet, there doesn't seem reason to believe such a theory is impossible.

In conclusion, Natsoulas touches on what he sees as the major reasons for discontent and criticism directed against Sperry's mind-brain theory from both science and religion: an inadequate understanding of the process of emergence and an unwarranted reliance on a premature stage of science.

> The functioning of the brain is not as mundane as think the critics who compare it with their highly meaningful and luxuriant mental phenomena. It is often such a comparison between something rich and vibrant and something else of an uninteresting basic simplicity that decides the question of whether experiences could be brain processes. I believe that such views simply reflect the historical point at which we find ourselves in our understanding of the brain.[22]

Ripley and Concern with Language

While Natsoulas concentrates on the task of finding responses to criticism of Sperry, Professor Charles Ripley concentrates on criticism of Sperry himself. In fact, from beginning to end, his paper on "Sperry's Concept of Consciousness" strings one point of dissatisfaction behind the other. Yet, Ripley's paper is not a criticism of Sperry's *philosophy;* it is a criticism of the scientist's "cavalier attitude to language," which invites misunderstanding. His philosophy is sincerely admired.

To unveil the true meaning of Sperry's thoughts, Ripley vigorously attacks their expression—all the while emphasizing his high regard for the *content* of Sperry's thoughts, which he terms "an exciting thesis of momentous import for philosophy and behavioral science."[23]

Ripley even excuses Sperry's "linguisitic infelicities" as "not entirely due to carelessness." Instead, he believes that the nature of language itself is partly at fault.

> That something is material, for instance, suggests that it is not mental; and if it is mental it is not material. . . . I have said that Sperry's locution "mental forces that transcend the material elements in cerebral function" is misleading; but what words ought he have used?[24]

We might add that there is one important aspect of Sperry's choice of language that Ripley does not seem to acknowledge: Sperry writes for the person with general knowledge, an open mind, and common sense, and he therefore must select words and connotations with which such a person is at home. He does not write for the analytical philosopher. Moreover, as the discoverer of unexpected right-hemisphere capabilities, Sperry naturally addresses himself in part to these—to intuitive and tacit understanding.

Although Ripley does not see that side of Sperry's work, his efforts to make the scientist's thoughts palatable to those who carry weight in the field of philosophy are of great value.

The following are among the issues that Ripley addresses:

1. Clarification of such "controversial" concepts as *holistic, systemic,* and *emergent* properties, which "in the present philosophical climate . . . are widely viewed with disfavour or suspicion"

2. Interpretation of Sperry's view as materialistic
3. Rejection of Sperry's position as a "midway compromise between the older extremes of mentalism on the one hand and materialism on the other"
4. Rejection of Sperry's term *interaction* in reference to the mind-brain relationship
5. Rejection of Sperry's belief that his position implies that values can be incorporated into neuro science, and even a questioning of Sperry's main tenet that science can be reconciled with the humanities.

That is a formidable list, indeed, and although Ripley's intent was to strengthen Sperry's position, some of his interpretations cannot possibly be accepted either by Sperry himself or by his supporters.

Let us return to each point in more detail.

As for point 1, Ripley's thorough treatment of such concepts as *holistic, systemic,* and *emergent* is successful in freeing these expressions from every vestige of the supernatural which they may have acquired in the past, before sufficient knowledge of the details involved in natural processes was available, and which may linger on in the minds of many philosophers.[25]

Ripley interprets Sperry's view as materialistic (point 2) based on a previous argument that mental events and physical events are two kinds of material events. He therefore interprets Sperry's theory as a psychophysical identity theory (that is, mind is identical to matter) and Sperry's position as materialistic. Appearances to the contrary are explained in terms of Sperry's "carelessness" in his use of language as well as difficulties inherent in language itself.

Ripley considers Sperry's description of his theory as a "midway compromise between older extremes of mentalism and materialism" (point 3) as another "unfortunate use of terms." The professor of psychology Dalbir Bindra objects to that compromise as inadmissible because the two positions are "logically incompatible." Ripley objects to it because they are *too* compatible: "mental forces *are* material; to describe them as transcending material elements (as Sperry has done) is to invite misunderstanding."

In terms of point 4, Ripley argues that Sperry's occasional reference to *interactionism* leads to the misinterpretation of his position as dualistic. This had already been discerned by Sperry himself, and he has since discontinued the use of that term.

It is not clear, however, how far Sperry would agree with Ripley's preceding two objections—points 2 and 3. It seems unlikely that Sperry's desire to be comprehensible to the mainstream of the population would permit him to speak of an identity of the mental and the material.

Moreover, is it really necessary to claim such an identity in order to differentiate Sperry's position from the supernatural? We do not think so. Although both matter and mind are part of our natural world, although both are intimately related to each other and never separate, they are nevertheless two different phenomena. However thoroughly one studies the physico-chemical events in a fellow-being's brain, his subjective experiences resulting from them will forever be inaccessible through such research alone. Subjective experience is an emergent of brain activity that opens a new dimension of reality. That dimension can not be encompassed by the word *material*.

Finally, Ripley rejects what Sperry considers the very core of his philosophy: its ability to merge the realms of science and values. For Sperry, the view that consciousness is an emergent phenomenon can reconcile science, values, and the humanities. The various guidelines, values, and precepts which animate the latter two areas of human thought are rooted, in the end, in human consciousness; and that, in turn, is something that science can elucidate and explain, through its exploration of the workings of the brain.

Ripley finds such claims unacceptable. Though the hoped-for reconciliation may be part of Sperry's theory, the grand results that Sperry expects—the merging of science, religion, and humanities into a single harmonious worldview—are extraordinarily dubious. Sperry's very claim that values can be incorporated into neuroscience is, says Ripley, a direct contradiction of Sperry's own principles. Sperry argues that values are a product of consciousness, and characteristic of it. Consciousness, in turn, is something that emerges from brain activity. The precise nature of that activity—how it gives rise to consciousness—is not yet known; but we assume that the answers will be found by neuroscientists as they learn more and more about the innermost workings of the brain. However, says Ripley, just because brain activity is the province of the neuroscientists does *not* mean that properties that emerge from brain activity, such as consciousness, are also best understood by neuroscientists using scientific methods. And further products of those emergent properties, such as values, are yet another step removed.

Ripley draws an analogy with physics. If we were searching for an expert on how the human brain works, we would not look for a nuclear physicist, despite the fact that the brain is composed of subatomic particles which nuclear physicists understand more thoroughly and completely than anyone else. But just because a nuclear physicist knows all there is to know about the parts that make up the brain doesn't mean he is an expert on how those parts behave when combined into a greater whole. By the same token, then, though neuroscientists may be experts on how the components of consciousness—neurons and systems of neurons—operate, the question of how those components are combined into a greater whole, and how that greater whole then creates constructions like values and morals, lies far beyond the province of neuroscience. Ripley concludes that Sperry's bid to incorporate values into science is without foundation and, in fact, "represents a lapse into reductionism that he elsewhere rejects."[26]

This is obviously a serious objection, one which, if sustained, would undercut any wider applicability of Sperry's theories to current global problems. Sperry's response is two-fold: first, he had never rejected reductionism, but only insisted that it must be *supplemented* by a holistic perspective; that is, physical and mental phenomena in the brain must be seen as results not only of events at the subatomic, atomic, and molecular levels but also of their organization through higher-level influences, such as conscious awareness. Second, science does determine values, insofar as facts (about the universe, life, man) change our beliefs about the world, causing us to reassess the values we hold.[27]

The truth of that is self-evident: for instance, after hormones were discovered, it became impossible to interpret the longing for sex in terms of sin and depravity. After neuroscientist Wilder Penfield caused patients to relive apparently long-lost memories by touching neural tissue with electrodes, the view of the mind as residing in a supernatural world of its own, untouched and uninfluenced by the body, faded more rapidly.

So we can see how brain science affects values. However, the relationship between values and brain science is two-sided: (1) The brain affects our conceptions and subsequent actions. For example, we cannot punish persons for their wrongdoing if it is understood to be caused through the malfunctioning of their brains (such as the result of brain tumors). (2) Consciousness affects activity in the brain, even while remaining a property of brain events, as Natsoulas helped to make clear. For instance, brain-functioning cannot be fully understood unless the higher guiding principles determining its overall coordination are taken into account. We cannot speak about these principles in the language of neuroscience, because that language does not cover the subjective experience which is an immanent part of brain events at the highest level. The language of neuroscience cannot provide us with a full and true account of what happens in the brain. Therefore, unless we speak in the language of the humanities, we cannot speak about the most important events in the brain at all. To describe mental events in the language of brain science alone would force us to treat one another as if our brains were not fully functional, as if we were demented.

Neuroscience informs us only about those aspects of neural

interactions that affect our instruments: our electrodes, our video displays, and so on. Subjective experience is far more precise and informative: it provides us with knowledge of detailed, specific effects of the internal and external environment upon our neuronal activity, and knowledge about the ongoing interactions of all these. Only that knowledge, infinitely more complete than any knowledge obtained through our instruments, makes adequate responses at the highest level of brain activity possible. The discovery that subjective experience is a more precise advisor about, and organizer of, brain events than anything we can learn through our instruments is tantamount to the ancient Egyptian discovery that the sky provides a more precise basis for a calendar than the floods of the Nile.

Sperry has both of these aspects in mind—the effect of brain events on consciousness and the effect of consciousness on brain events—when he speaks about the relationship between values and brain science, but the second aspect is his special contribution. It embodies the original and significant content of his mind-brain theory and his related philosophy of ethics.

Although Sperry was forced to single out that second side of the brain-value relationship—the effect of mind on matter—to draw attention to a long overlooked and prominent aspect of reality, both sides are of equal importance. Science and values are intimately related. But a "new science" is needed—more precisely a new philosophy of science—that would make this interrelationship seem natural. If we restrict ourselves to our traditional way of thinking, with its little watertight compartments of knowledge, this new science appears out of place everywhere. An ordained minister might declare brain science to be part of religion, using arguments about the brain-value relationship similar to those of Sperry; and he would encounter the same puzzlement among his colleagues that Sperry encounters in the field of science.

Rational decision making will thus remain awkward and cumbersome until the grand vista accessible now only to a few becomes part of our common human perception of reality.

Rottschaefer and Values from Science

Philosopher William A. Rottschaefer disagrees with Charles Ripley's conclusion (discussed earlier) that one cannot derive values from science. According to Rottschaefer, Sperry's *emergent mentalism* succeeds in dealing with what were thought to be insuperable obstacles to creating a science-based ethos. As Rottschaefer sees it, the reason why Sperry's theory succeeds where others have failed is clear.

> It does so because it recognizes from the perspective of the neurosciences the crucial role of the mental in any account of the genealogy and justification of values. Supplemented by non-reductionistic socio-biological and behavioral accounts of values, as well as contributions from the social sciences, it opens up the possibility of the account of the origin, development and maintenance of values ranging from the genetic to the socio-cultural.[28]

But Rottschaefer believes that Sperry's value theory fails to bridge what he calls the "prescriptive-justificatory gap"—in other words, it cannot *prescribe* or *justify* what values we should adhere to. As Rottschaefer sees it, Sperry's theory is short of the one crucial component that his own theory supplies: the requirement that any course of action be one that "fulfills human capacities."[29]

However, we would argue that Sperry's theory *does* bridge this crucial gap by presenting as humanity's highest goal the "preserving and enhancing of an ever evolving quality of existence." That goal does not stand in contrast to the one suggested by Rottschaefer, nor does it bridge the fact-value gap only partially, as Rottschaefer believes. Rather, it is Sperry's goal that is the more encompassing one, the one that includes, but is not restricted to, what "fulfills human capacities."

Slaatte and the Creativity of Consciousness

The philosopher of science and religion Howard A. Slaatte also agrees with Sperry's point of view that science and values can and should be merged, and he enthusiastically supports Sperry's efforts in that region. Slaatte opens the second chapter of his book *The Creativity of Consciousness*, discussing Sperry's work, with the following words:

> Developments in psychobiology in recent years bespeak a near breakthrough to the human mind. The reason for this is that a scientific methodology and a holistic psychology centering around the role of consciousness are reconciled for the first time in history.[30]

Slaatte comes to Sperry's philosophy from both a left-hemisphere and a right-hemisphere perspective, concerned with both its analytical and its holistic, integrating aspects. For him, as for Ripley, "any dichotomy of the mental and the physical has to be questioned," yet he does not therefore insist that Sperry's is a materialistic position. Instead, Slaatte refuses either to reduce one level of organization to a lower one or to elevate a lower level without justification. He emphasizes that Sperry's theory of mind supports his own conviction that consciousness is a unique phenomenon which expresses the coexistence of "both [the] continuity and qualitative discontinuity" of biological and mental events.

> Dependent upon the cerebral mechanism, the conscious mind functions from within them, but it does so to the extent of actually influencing them. . . . The functions are distinguishable while interrelated.[31]

In short, mind is born *of* matter, but different *from* matter. Going beyond *emergence* and *causality*, Slaatte uses the beautiful word *creativity* to describe the function of the mind.

> A green image, for instance, has no place in the physics of the phenomenons . . . the color and brain process per se do not correspond fully. The experience is a kind of interpretation based on the combination of the physical and the conscious levels. . . . Consciousness is emergent and creative. What it observes to be a

green object is its very own observation, so to speak, while drawing upon the sensations proffered it by the physical mechanism,
and, in turn, that which are their stimuli. The fallacy of a naive
realism is thus overcome by the two-in-one interrelationship . . .
that spells not only correlation but uniqueness.[32] (Italics added.)

Through his description of how the mind "creates" the color
"green," Slaatte leads us to understand how it creates such abstracts as "meaning," "purpose," "ideals," and "values." He
would agree not only with the generally accepted assumption
that the experience of consciousness coincides with the creation of a correlated brain pattern acting as a whole but also with
the further contention that without the correlated conscious
qualities, organization of brain processing at conscious levels
could not take place.

Like Sperry, Slaatte is dissatisfied with a worldview in which
consciousness has no place. Like Sperry, he cannot prove his
assumptions about the uniqueness of consciousness. Yet opposing theories that have always assumed consciousness to be superfluous cannot prove their tenets either; and they are far less
likely to provide a valid description of reality.

In any case, progress in our understanding of the world does
not always begin with proven facts; but it inevitably requires
imagination and courage—the courage to send intuition out
into uncharted regions, the courage to state one's conjectures,
to defend them, and to submit them to criticism.

Transformation of a Discipline

The evidence of consciousness and reasoning could be explained in other
ways in animals, why not also in man?
—B. F. Skinner

It is in the light of these decades of *denial* of consciousness as causal reality
that Roger Sperry's pronouncement comes with such impact. It is similar
to the impact of Copernicus' theories after centuries of denying that the
Earth, being the assumed center of the universe and special focus of divine attention, could possibly move.
—Willis Harman

A wide shift of attitudes took place in the late 1960s and early 1970s in the behavioral sciences—a transformation that is now entering neuroscience, evolutionary biology, and related areas. Materialistic, mechanistic, and behaviorist views were swept aside and replaced by theories allowing consciousness into the worldview of science. The shift continues, and this book is dedicated to its acceleration.

Colwyn Trevarthen of the University of Edinburgh, one of Sperry's former graduate students and postdoctoral fellows, wrote in 1990:

> Reflection on the manifestations of conscious awareness in the surgically divided brain led Sperry, in 1965, to publish the first of a remarkable series of philosophical papers. . . . Though greeted with some skepticism initially, this mentalist view of consciousness based on emergence and downward causation was destined within 10 years to replace behaviorism as the dominant foundational philosophy of behavioral science.[33]

On the whole, mentalism supplanted behaviorism silently; the movement seemed to lack highly visible leaders. Nearly all the scientists involved in the shift of paradigm attributed it to a shift in their inner convictions rather than to external causes. The many causes for this new and liberating atmosphere, of which Sperry's work now seems to have been among the most influential, were not pursued to their roots.

Where credit is given to Sperry's influence, however, it is usually enthusiastic. For example, Ralph W. Lewis of Michigan State University calls Sperry's theory of consciousness "the most important theory set forth in the last few decades";[34] the eminent Canadian academic Charles Ripley, whose ideas we have already considered, calls Sperry's thesis "exciting . . . of momentous import for philosophy and behavioral science" and even "of revolutionary import";[35] and the neuroscientist and Nobel laureate David H. Hubel expresses the conviction that

Sperry's contributions "represent a revolution in science comparable to the Copernican revolution or the Darwinian revolution."[36] Sperry himself, however, trying to trace the many and diverse causes of this transformation of the behavioral sciences, points to a vast array of sources:

new developments in computer science, artificial intelligence, and information theory

the rise to prominence of cognitive psychology, which emphasizes the study of brain and thought processes, rather than external behavior

Gestalt psychology, which is built on the central assumption that wholes are more than simply the sum of their parts

humanistic psychology

new findings on the nature of mental imagery and perception

inadequacies in some aspects of behaviorism which have become steadily more apparent

the new philosophy dominating cognitive science, which emphasizes the importance of mental and functional aspects of cognitive phenomena

the work of Carl Rogers and Abraham Maslow

"consciousness raising" movements

the counterculture movement of the late 1960s, which was in part a reaction against the traditional materialism and reductionism of twentieth-century science and technology

insights drawn from general systems theory

the contributions of such thinkers as Karl Popper, Noam Chomsky (who pioneered a new and seminal view of language learning), Sigmund Koch, Stanley Stevens, Jerome Bruner, Edward Tolman, Jerry Fodor, and Hilary Putnam insights provided by the phenomenological school of psychology, which studies the conscious experience of phenomena

There are many others, among them particularly the physical chemist and social philosopher Michael Polanyi, whose views Sperry considers closest to his own.[37]

But as Sperry untangled the innumerable branches of intertwisting ideas, he found one concept, "the appearance in the 1960s of an emergent, functional, interactionist concept of consciousness that gives subjective mental phenomena a causal role in brain processing and behavior," to be the essential factor that transformed an entire discipline. None of the other influences would have been incompatible with the materialistic and behavioristic views that then dominated the behavioral sciences.

> Whereas the basic behaviorist philosophy of science could be adjusted to accommodate advances in computer simulation, information theory, cognitive process research, linguistic and other cognitive developments in the 1960s, behaviorism could not adapt to a new concept of consciousness as causal. The two views, at bedrock, are mutually exclusive and irreconcilable.[38]

If the concept of consciousness as causal, which seemed outrageous in the early 1960s and is now generally accepted, proves more than a passing fad, the "Consciousness Revolution" may in fact be compared with the Darwinian and Copernican revolutions. Yet there is a critical difference. Those revolutions tilted our notion of reality toward a mechanistic worldview, led to fears that our values may vanish, and provoked vigorous countermovements toward the renewal of literal belief in the Bible. Including consciousness, ideas, and ideals in a scientific worldview, however, will have the opposite result. Values will become an integral aspect of our conception of reality. A one-world view acceptable to both science and religion will be born; arguments against science as well as religion will lose their foundation.

That this transformation will be more than a passing fad has become increasingly apparent. The idea of consciousness as emergent and causal is now accepted and promoted in the world of the hard sciences itself—by, for instance, Nobel laureate Gerald Edelman, who entered the area from the field of microbiology. His investigations of the mind-brain problem are detailed, thorough, and solidly based in neuroscience—and they support Sperry's trailblazing work and visions point for point. Like Sperry, Edelman maintains that to study the brain while leaving out any mention of consciousness is to omit what is most crucial. Like Sperry, he believes that we must approach the problem from an evolutionary perspective; that "extreme reductionist positions that expect to account for consciousness on the basis of quantum mechanics . . . seem overambitious and empty";[39] that consciousness is generated by the "pattern properties" of neural networks; that it helps direct neural activity in the brain; and so on. Even behaviorism is rejected by both. Although Edelman, unlike Sperry, speaks of consciousness as a *physical* rather than a mental phenomenon because it emerges from the functioning of the physical brain, no fundamental difference exists between the two positions. Nor can Edelman avoid concluding that consciousness cannot be treated adequately without taking account of philosophy and metaphysics.

What Sperry proposed in the 1960s finds now, in the 1990s, step-by-step support by mainstream science. There is but one important difference. The very same phenomenon, consciousness—emerging from the workings of the brain, directing the activity of the neurons, imposing on them an overarching pattern of activity—is described as a "physical" phenomenon by mainstream science because it emerges from the activity of the *physical* brain.[40] Sperry, on the other hand, prefers the term *mental*, because this phenomenon differs fundamentally from any material entity. Consciousness exists in dramatic contrast to anything previously produced by evolution.

And, too, Sperry uses the adjective *mental* in the sense that it has been used throughout history: to refer to the subjective world of ideas, experiences, and emotions. Because a world of connotation and meaning is conjured up by *mental* that is absent in *physical*, the difference is more than a question of mere labels. In effect, Sperry is trying to build a bridge between two worlds, hoping to join the "new world" of science to an "old world" encompassing centuries of humanistic gifts. As well, he hopes that religionists will be attracted rather than repelled by this new description of reality.

The question of how Sperry's theory of values has been received in both religion and the humanities, of which barriers remain and why, and of how these barriers can be removed will be the topic of our next chapter.

·9·
Toward Right-Hemisphere Acceptance

With what may be called the radical passion one must have sympathy. The passion to eliminate poverty, misery, hunger, malnutrition, and avoidable ill health, and to create a world in which every human being born has a reasonable opportunity to fulfill the genetic potential for health and learning, love and joy, grief and resignation, is a passion in tune with the potential of the human race. But we have to admit, however unwillingly and unpleasantly, that passion is frequently but not necessarily the enemy of truth, and that passion distorts our image of the world often to the point where our illusions prevent fulfillment of the passion. It is the radical illusions, not the conservative coldness, that are the greatest enemies of the radical passion. If the radical passion is to be fulfilled, if we are indeed to move into a world that is better than what we have now, the radical illusions must be discarded and a realistic appraisal of the dynamic effects of human action must become widespread.
        —Kenneth Boulding

Merging Emotion and Reason

Can a person born with the gift of scientific reasoning, educated to sharpen and refine that gift, reinforced by his success in science in his utmost respect for it, find words to appeal to the hearts of those whose lives are shaped largely by their emotions? Can his thoughts find their way into the world of persons born with the gift of sensitivity to the feelings of their fellow-beings, educated with and for love and compassion, absorbed in the world of religion? Will not what may seem to the scientist a minor adjustment of a belief system appear to the devout believer the destruction of his world?

During his Isthmus Lecture in 1983—one of a series of lectures by Nobel laureates at the Isthmus Institute on Religion in Dallas, Texas—Sperry proposed what might seem for a scientist an extremely generous compromise: "Religion on the one side gives up dependence upon dualistic concepts, while science, on the other, gives up much of its traditional materialistic legacy including behavioristic, reductionistic, probalistic, mechanistic and deterministic principles." He suggested this "two-way compromise" as an improvement over the one-sided approach of traditional science which simply asks that "religion mend its ways to better conform with the facts and worldview of science."[1]

To an uninvolved referee, the compromise may sound fair, but is it something a religious believer could accept?

Perhaps the compromise would be easier to accept if, instead of asking religionists to abandon dualism, they were asked to "transfer" longing for a better life in the hereafter to longing for a decent life in the future, to "transfer" concern for a person's soul after death to concern for his soul living on in his descendants. The emotions and passions could then be retained in all their purity, unhurt and unspoiled, while reason might find relief in accepting a more valid and updated image of reality.

In fact, Sperry moves into this direction, especially in the later pages of the same paper, in which he proposes his "transfer." There he suggests that "the importance of religion fulfilling personal emotional needs and life meaning . . . would not need to be deemphasized or lost but only retargeted into this-world reality."[2]

A person trained in traditional religion and philosophy will also find it almost impossible to give up a belief in absolute values. Yet that is what the scientific conception of a changing and evolving universe demands. One of the students in Sperry's psychobiology class at Caltech provided insight into these difficulties on her "critical question card," a card each class member had to fill in weekly.

1. Sperry claims that "values in general, *by nature,* are not absolute but always relative to some context or frame of reference, involving often some implicitly accepted aim or intent" (p. 45). How can he consider this to be a "basic and important principle" when for thousands of years mankind has struggled toward the exact opposite, this is, toward establishing some "ultimate" frame of reference that, by nature, has value and meaning in itself? Values are, in the history of human thought, exactly those things that are not relative but *absolute.*

2. Sperry seems convinced (p. 47) that "the new holist-mentalist paradigm stands for something that is no longer in conflict with ethical, religious, or other humanist sensitivities": How can a world view that would seem to justify abortion, capital punishment and despotism (p. 49, first 6 lines), not be in conflict with ethical "sensitivities"? How can a theory that denies God, separate existence of soul outside the body and the possibility of a "personal" God (i.e. loving, caring, fatherly) not be in conflict with religion? How does a theory that does not grant value to the individual human being for its own intrinsic worth not offend human "sensitivities"?

This theory seems to me in direct conflict with these on their own foundations.

This is quoted with permission of the student, who prefers to remain anonymous because the point of view presented was not her own. She stated these arguments only as a basis for discussion, although in fact she is much impressed by Sperry's philosophy and shares his views. The pages cited refer to Sperry's book *Science and Moral Priority;* the first six lines of page 49 read:

These changes need not affect the entire citizenry, only those leaders involved in forming global policy. Scientific standards for validity are chosen, not with the idea that scientific truth is absolute or infallible, but only on the belief that it represents the best and most reliable, credible and dependable *approach to truth* available.

In this passage, "these changes" refer to the acceptance of "criteria for ultimate value" that are "required to jibe with scientific reality," which would mean for communist countries "some updating in interpretations of science and what science stands for, including a philosophic shift from materialism to mentalism" and for other countries "replacing or reconciling various otherworldly guidelines with this-world existence."

This is the despotism to which the student referred—a small elite's imposing of a new value system on an uncomprehending and perhaps even unsuspecting world. Is there no way around this? To be sure, Sperry could have inserted "at the outset" between "need" and "not affect." Of course, laws will be resisted without the previous or simultaneous education of the citizenry. To be effective *and* to avoid the danger of "despotism," that education must take full cognizance of reality. (Population problems provide one instance of this. As we see it, however, overpopulation cannot possibly be accepted as the only factor responsible for all global problems, while all excesses of greed are overlooked.)

But Sperry did not insert that crucial phrase "at the outset," leaving the charge of advocating despotism undismissed. Why? He understands the mental pain involved in changing a system of beliefs to which persons have been dedicated since their earliest years, and he sees no need for the majority of the population to be submitted to that pain.

Yet, benign dictatorship is not the only way. An alternative to pain and ignorance exists. It is possible to find simple, warm, and caring words to convert persons with little education and little attraction to critical thinking from one belief system to another, better one, if one has the ability to enter their mental world and to work from within it. For instance, a wonderful booklet with deep insights expressed in unpretentious everyday language, even using pictures and examples from the Bible, has recently been written by Carl Casebolt. *A Polaris for the Spirit* compares our need to adjust our values to changing conditions while retaining an ultimate reference point to early navigators' use of the polestar as guidance when tossed about in the open sea. The process of evolution and emergence is described as

"the marvellous and quiet way in which life moves forward to
fulfillment as though directed by an inner force or compulsion";
among his list of recent changes to which we must adjust are
energy problems, overpopulation, alternative life-styles, and
the threat of nuclear war. Our search must be for values "which
deal directly with reality" that are consistent "with science and
the highest religious insights." Casebolt explains that "one of
the gifts of modern theology has been to enlarge our conception
of God to include the definition of God as the structure of reality," and he believes that the separation of God from nature and
reality is an error:

> Many people . . . have come to an awareness that, even if we reject
> certain ideas about God, we cannot abolish or reject the ground
> of being or the structure of reality. High religion and science are
> not incompatible. Religion should have no quarrel with accurate
> descriptions of reality; science does not oppose the elevation of
> the human spirit. An adequate moral guide should reflect this
> view. . . . We should be able to derive new insights from a "Polaris
> of the Spirit" to meet the problems of our time.[3]

For Casebolt, our ultimate value, or "Polaris for the Spirit,"
consists of "concern for the fulfillment of life," because it goes
"beyond reverence for life to a concern for its quality."

Many far more sophisticated theological treatises show less
insight than this small and simple booklet, which moreover
manages to find within the general "upward thrust of evolution" a more specific direction which it is good to encourage. It
is a booklet that has the potential to reduce much of the fundamental opposition to Sperry's views on the part of traditional
religion. It is a booklet that mediates between two worlds
through its warmth and simplicity, a warmth and simplicity
that seems for many people incompatible with greatness, yet
which is such a large and appealing part of the vision of a personal God.

I do not have Casebolt's gifts of expression. I can only answer
the student's questions with thought-provoking counterques-

tions, in the hope that through discussion greater insight will emerge.

(1) Question: "How can a world view that would seem to justify abortion, capital punishment and despotism not be in conflict with ethical 'sensitivities'?" Counterquestions: How can we appeal to ethical sensitivities to avoid abortion, capital punishment and despotism, while closing our eyes to these sensitivities when we know that population pressure would make famine, plague, and mass murder of the most horrible kind an unavoidable fate? How can traditional ethical commands remain viable when they conflict with the ever more convincing successes of the scientific method? How can religion itself be saved from extinction unless it is updated to incorporate scientific truth?

(2) Question: "How can a theory that denies God, separate existence of soul outside the body, and the possibility of a 'personal' God (i.e., loving, caring, fatherly) not be in conflict with religion?" Counterquestions: How can a loving and caring father provide us with the gift of thought, foresight, and insight and then forbid us to act according to conclusions resulting from these? How can a loving and caring father permit us insight into the fact that the world around us is changing and then demand that we cling to absolute values suitable only for stationary conditions? How can thousands of years of mental struggle have relevance to insights elicited only through the threat of nuclear warfare?

(3) Question: "How does a theory that does not grant value to the individual human being for his own intrinsic worth not offend human 'sensitivities'?" Counterquestions: How could the intrinsic worth of a human being be separated from the intrinsic worth of the creation itself that produced him? Or, in the language of traditional religion: love and respect for man as the image of God and for God himself demands love and respect for his entire creation, because he is immanent in every being. Or, in the language of science: we have been created through the laws of the universe, and our health and well-being depend

upon the understanding of, and regard for, these laws; we cannot destroy our environment without mental and physical impoverishment.

Moreover, in Sperry's view, God is not denied but equated with the creative forces of the universe. Such a God is far greater, far more majestic, than the one described in traditional religion; and most importantly, he becomes more credible. Even the most convinced atheist cannot disobey the laws of nature except at his own peril. Yet the personal, loving, caring, and fatherly aspect of God has not vanished, because with the emergence of man, nature also created his emotions, his longings, his ideals, and his aspirations. All these are part of our reality, part of our universe, part of our creator. Instead of vanishing, God's concern too becomes more real. Experienced not as outside us but as within, God, through our own decisions, may transform Monod's "frozen universe of solitude" into a home— independently of any other person's attitudes toward us. For if we love, with the depth of our being and without calculation, then our world is not empty of God's love; and if we care, with our mind and our heart and our thoughts and our deeds, then our world is not empty of God's care.

Nor will our souls vanish after death. Parts of ourselves are imprinted forever on our gifts to mankind, are living in our descendants, are embodied in our actions and their consequences. These, it may be objected, are not our souls at all; they are the *products* of conscious experience, not the experience itself. Nevertheless, in them the highest expressions of our experiences are made eternal. Sperry would consider these expressions of our inner life—whether they be symphonies or scientific papers—of greater importance than the fleeting passage of everyday subjective impressions.

We can perhaps not find a better treatment, from the point of view of science, of the relationship between life and death, and the question of the eternal life of the soul, than in Sperry's own words. As a scientist, of course, Sperry does not use the word *soul*—an old fashioned and strictly religious expression originating before the mind-brain connection was known and still trailing vague visions of ghost-like shadows. Instead, he uses the terms *the conscious self,* or *conscious experience,* the equivalent of the scientist's concept of the mind.

Sperry shares philosopher Karl Popper's belief that death enhances the meaning and significance of life, in much the same way, he suggests, that a bout of sickness helps us appreciate good health. Imagining that there is a "better beyond and an eternal hereafter" only diminishes the value of the most sophisticated and complex product of eons of evolution—human consciousness. If we are convinced that we are only passing through this existence on our way through heaven or hell, we tend to see this life as only a "way station."

Of course, what makes us fear death—and deny its very existence—is the prospect that after but a few short years, we are consigned to oblivion. Our individual conscious existences are but fleeting sparks in a universe vast and ancient—mere fireflies in an infinite night. Can science offer us any solace?

Sperry's answer seems to be at least a conditional yes. Pragmatically it may be possible to save something of "the conscious self in its very highest form" after physical death occurs. If we adopt an emergent view of how the human mind is produced by brain activity, then what would be the most important properties to preserve? "Not the atomic, molecular, or physiological infrastructure," Sperry replies, "but rather the supersedent mental events, forces and properties, *per se.*" And if we were to decide which thoughts, experiences, and events make us most truly human—which are, in Sperry's phrase, "the most highly evolved"—then surely it would not be those thoughts associated with the mundane fabric of daily life. It would be the "special peaks" that we would pick out; and, moreover, it would not be the pattern of brain activity producing these peaks that we would want to salvage, but instead, "the transcendental mental content itself"—the very distillation of the best that has ever been thought or said.

But in that case, do we not already live on after death in some sense?

> Perhaps the essence of the very best of the conscious self of Beethoven, or Shakespeare, Michelangelo, and the like are still with us. We cannot all be Beethovens, of course, or Leonardos, or Edisons, or Darwins, but there are ways in which the highest aspect or form of the conscious experiences of each individual can realistically be extended in this manner to exist beyond death of the neural substrate that originally sustained it.[4]

This new unifying view of science and religion does not debase religion or reduce it to insignificance; it invigorates religion, infusing it with new credibility, new sacredness, new life.

Although scientists will fully agree with Sperry, many devout believers will feel that these explanations are insufficient, and that they fail to approach the inner peace and happiness provided by belief in an unembodied self in the final and eternal care of the Almighty. The human soul resides neither in "everyday thoughts" nor in the material products of peak experiences. It resides in these peak experiences themselves: in the experience of the divine, in the expression of the divine, in the feeling of communion with the divine.

But there is a way in which even the devoutly religious person may transcend his concern with the unembodied self, not through the rejection of his or her belief, but through experiencing the divine at a more fundamental level, unchained from any dogma or specific belief system. During that experience, the individual meets the divine in depth and in truth, becoming one with the universe. All its separate, distracting aspects vanish. It no longer matters whether the entity once known as "I" remains alive after death: all that matters is the overwhelming sensation of a love that knows no boundaries. The quest for the life of an individual soul after death becomes immaterial.

Here believers in all the religions of the world, be they of the West or the East—and even those confessing no faith at all—are unified during moments of their deepest experience.

Now let us turn to the practical aspect of religion: the guidance of human decision making. What should be done if short-term and long-term concerns conflict?

In his foreword to Sperry's *Science and Moral Priority,* Colwyn Trevarthen writes about Sperry's ethics: "His arguments demand that more 'godlike perspectives,' referent to all creation, be placed above otherwise compelling humanitarian rules of conduct when the two appear in conflict." That aspect of Sperry's moral priorities is certainly the most unacceptable from the point of view of religion. Although it is true that God himself, even in the traditional understanding as a loving and caring father, often acts for the long-range good in ways beyond human scrutiny, and although a predominant part of the task of religious leaders consists in explaining apparent gross injustices as part of a long-term beneficial plan, it seems impossible to accept that man himself—man with his limited mental abilities and limited power of prediction—should willfully commit short-term brutalities to avoid worse disasters in the future.

During one of the psychobiology classes I attended under Sperry, I asked the question: "Does long-term concern necessarily imply short-term brutality if both are in conflict?"

As was the custom in these classes—Sperry was convinced that the students most eager to speak were not necessarily those with the most important contributions to make—names of those who had to answer were drawn through a lottery, and answers came slowly and reluctantly: "Yes, I think so . . ."; "I believe we have to . . ."; "I can see no other way . . ." When answers from anyone else were invited, there was complete silence. Finally, I asked for permission to answer my own question.

> We cannot condone brutality [I said] and remain human. Instead, we have to direct all our intelligence, all our efforts, to alternative solutions of such conflicts wherever they occur. Anesthetics have been invented to make operations possible without pain; birth control pills have been invented to reduce both short- and long-

term unhappiness and misery. Similarly, every conflict between present and future must be treated as a problem to be solved through our ingenuity.

That answer, of course, is not very helpful unless and until alternative solutions *have* been found. In the meantime, in making such decisions, one must take the entire situation into account, no doubt deciding sometimes in favor of short-term and sometimes of long-term humanitarian concerns. Questions such as the following must be asked: How valid is the long-term projection? How severe is the suffering we cause now in comparison to what we would avoid later? Is not much of what is now conceived as "good" actually the most inhumane cruelty? Many other questions will have to be asked—and answered—before the right balance between short-term and long-term considerations can be struck. Although more concern with long-term goals is urgently necessary, to pay for them with our humanity would be too expensive. *Absolute* moral priorities may lead to the same problems as absolute moral precepts, and conflicts must always first and foremost be perceived as challenges to our ingenuity.

For the scientist, who is convinced that *no one* guides our fate or foresees the future, the task is straightforward. He looks at the facts, such as:

> In southern India 45,000 children under 14 years are working, mostly in factories. One girl of age 3½ was found working in a match factory. The poverty is so terrible that people have nothing but their labour to give in exchange for goods.[5]

He then concludes that overpopulation reduces the quality of life severely and should be avoided by all possible means for humanitarian reasons.

He may also consider what both science and history tell us about that feared grim reaper of the Middle Ages that still stalks the world today: plague. A quick glance at the encyclopedia reveals the dread statistics. The Black Death and the bubonic plague (both caused by the same microorganism) start with nausea, joint aches, and a burning fever, which may soar as high as 105 degrees Fahrenheit. The victim's lymph nodes swell—sometimes to the size of chicken eggs—and poisons produced by the disease spread through the entire body, weakening the kidneys, heart, and causing swelling of the brain. Delirium, restlessness, light-headedness, even mania may occur. The time between infection and death may be as little as three to four days.

If the plague bacterium attacks the victim's lungs, *primary pneumonic plague* develops. Phlegm and blood are coughed up, and the gap between the first symptoms and death is often only forty-eight hours.

In the Black Death, the hemorrhages of the stricken are literally black in colour—hence the name.

The disease is harbored by populations of rats, then carried from rats to humans by fleas. If the pneumonia form develops, however, the coughing victim spreads the disease even more easily and insidiously.

Reports of the plague date back at least to an outbreak in Greece in the fifth century before Christ. The most disastrous incidence of the disease ever recorded started in 1334 in Constantinople and spread throughout Asia and Europe. Before it was over more than one-third—some authorities say as much as three-quarters—of the population was dead. Outbreaks of the plague continued into modern times, and, indeed, even today it is still found in underdeveloped regions of the world, though modern medicine and sanitation can prevent epidemics from spreading.[6]

The scientist closes the encyclopedia and puts it back on the bookshelf. Controlling population through noninterference with the time-tested methods of nature, he decides, is definitely not the right answer.

Finally, he may come across some literature on the consequences of nuclear warfare and read:

In the wake of nuclear war, epidemics will be reactivated, while survivors' resistance will be down. Our imagination fails to visualize the heat and blast effects, and we do not want to face the knowledge. Hiroshima and Nagasaki are almost nothing compared to what is in store for us now—yet that experience is a horror we don't want to face. . . . No doctor can tell radiation sickness in the early stages. The blood-generating system is the first affected by radiation. Babies are born microcephalic (with small heads)—mentally retarded, if they were exposed to radiation in utero.[7]

By now thoroughly shaken (if he has a conscience at all)—and thinking about the thousands of Ph.D.s who labored to increase the effectiveness of nuclear weapons—our scientist is convinced that trust in high I.Q. alone is insufficient.

He concludes that we need values to guide our intelligence, and that traditional values have become inadequate, because they lack credibility and because they prevent effective solutions. We need new values, incorporating the fact-based knowledge of science, but guided by our striving to become more humane.

For the religious fundamentalist, the person who takes the Bible literally and who believes that unshakable absolute values were set down thousands of years ago at the behest of God, the process is far more difficult. His confidence in a superhuman provider leads him to believe that, in spite of all appearances to the contrary, an all-wise, all-good God cares for our fate, and human attempts to interfere with his wisdom, or even to think independently, are not only useless but sacrilegious. He will readily interpret all the world's evils as failure to adhere to God's commands—but never, *never* question these commands themselves. To admit that a too literal adherence to an ancient creed might degrade and destroy the only species to consciously exercise love and compassion that has ever evolved (at least here on earth)—that it might obliterate the very existence of these sacred concepts—would be heresy.

To address this problem with cynicism, or even with cold reason, would make it worse. But simple words, appealing to emotions and transmitting wisdom with warmth and compassion, may be able to melt away barriers against a possible prevention of our peril.

One important first step would be to remove the traditional, erroneous understanding of evolution as destructive of religion and to replace it by a more updated and realistic one: evolution provided us with empathy and concern for one another—the fertile soil in which religion took root.

Toward a More Profound Understanding of Evolution

The record of the earth abounds in successful examples of partnership, starting early in the algal mats in which much of the earth's life was embedded, in mutual dependent layers, more than a billion years ago.
—Lewis Thomas

Competition plays an obvious role in nature, and many improvements would not have been achieved without it. Its existence is the first and most striking observation we make about relations among living organisms. Only later and more careful studies have discovered the much larger role played by compatible relationships, symbiosis, and so forth.[8] At the human level, the development of the intellect has depended upon an unusual amount of concern and care; all the higher achievements of culture have been founded upon the mind's ability to carve out for itself a realm above mere animal aims and passions. In an age of nuclear and chemical weapons, mass warfare, and an intricately interdependent world economy, it would be suicidal to promote competition as *the* command of nature. Did not nature itself create the human mind to make intelligent choices or, where all choices would be equally unsatisfactory, to invent alternatives?[9]

Sperry himself distinguishes and distances his philosophy in many of his papers from accusations of *social Darwinism,* Herbert Spencer's Victorian conception of (in Tennyson's phrase) "nature red in tooth and claw."

He has called on humanity to look to "higher values above those of material self-interest, economic gain, politics, production power, daily needs for personal subsistence, . . . to higher, more long term, more godlike priorities."[10] Nature, in his view, includes "mental, cultural, and other human and social forces . . . which are full of purpose, personal caring, value and meaning."[11]

The insight that rivalry must not be overrated is defended even by such tough-minded persons as Garrett Hardin. Lack of competition leads to stagnation; too much of it to extinction. An optimum level, leading to improvement, lies in between.[12]

Not the degree of competition, however, but its quality is most important. Never must the hunger for power be allowed to destroy those values which make us human: concern, empathy, integrity, among others.

Moreover, one crucial difference between man and lower organisms must never be forgotten: the unequaled extent of human individuality. No two humans are alike, and our everyday life is a patchwork of millions of decisions and choices. Making reasonable decisions depends on having a reality-oriented belief system. Without it, we have no hope.

Many experts on lower organisms, preoccupied as they are with subhuman species, have trouble appreciating the extent of human individuality and its unique gifts and demands. The well-known professor of bacterial physiology Bernard D. Davis is an exception. He recently drew attention to the limitations of approaching ethics from the point of view of biology.

> It is impossible to foresee how far sociobiology and neurobiology will go in improving our ethical systems and in promoting their acceptance. But we must recognize limits. Biology can provide firm facts and can reveal underlying mechanisms, but these are only a foundation. Not only for those who feel a need to invoke the transcendent but equally for those who do not, the biological description of human nature can only be coarse grained: Analysis of gene-environment interactions is no substitute for such concepts as poetry, inspiration, and love.[13]

Such insights are absent in the worldview of too many scientists, as well as nonscientists influenced by them.

Even Sperry's conception of a Grand Design of Nature as our guiding precept can result in difficulties, for the Grand Design lends itself to two different and contrasting interpretations when it comes time to formulate practical guidelines.[14]

The first interpretation is that ruthless and relentless competition among humans, as promoted by adherents to a gross misunderstanding of nonhuman nature, is right and good. According to this view, the forward thrust of evolution demands that we use our intelligence to surge ahead of competitors by all possible means—even by deceit, if it can be used covertly enough to avoid detection and retribution. Human compassion and empathy are aberrations which led to the problem of overpopulation in the first place, and all other problems, such as pollution, depletion of natural resources, and the threat of nuclear warfare, are only consequences of that paramount dilemma.

The second interpretation is that ruthless and relentless competition among humans, as promoted by adherents to a gross misunderstanding of nonhuman nature, is an evil because it will necessarily lead to the destruction of the highest achievement of evolution itself, the capacity for love and compassion in human nature. According to that view, the problem of overpopulation and its ensuing consequences arises only if love and compassion dominate to the exclusion of reason and foresight, as in many traditional religions. In this second interpretation, attention is paid to the fact that the greatest forward leaps in evolution have been achieved not through competition but through cooperation.

Matter, as we know it, was created when subatomic particles combined into atoms; life was created when certain atoms and molecules happened to find the right constellation to form self-replicating cells; multicellular organisms and their resulting consciousnesses or minds arose through the right form of inter-

action among some of these cells. At present, we are struggling
to find a new constellation among organisms that would lead
to a worldwide, livable, multiorganismic society.

The first interpretation of evolution is wrong, and it will lead
to the destruction of mankind and possibly of all life on earth.
Competition fierce enough to include ruthlessness and deceit
leads necessarily to mistrust, fear, and desperate countermea-
sures. Within nations, it leads to the horrors of concentration
camps, where many of the most valuable contributors to the
welfare of mankind are degraded and eliminated by their more
ruthless compatriots. Between nations, it leads to the even more
horrible fate of nuclear warfare.

Many persons believe that either totalitarian repression or
nuclear Armageddon is man's fate. We do not agree. The second
interpretation of evolution, if clearly incorporated into Sperry's
Grand Design and vigorously emphasized, will lead to a general
acceptance of that design as a framework for our values, and
through it to a viable global society, a society in which not intelligence alone, and not good will toward man alone, but both
would be equally influential. We must understand that such
good will, empathy, and mutual regard are necessary if we are
to draw together to solve our problems, which have increased
to such formidable size that no single person, not even the most
outstanding one, can solve them alone.

To those who believe with the sociobiologists that striving for
dominance is an innate motivation, so deeply embedded in human nature that it cannot be changed, we say: we know that
empathy with one another and regard for one another are also
part of human nature. Our motivations compete, and we must
choose among them.

Since prehistoric times religion has had to mediate among
competing motivations and to select those compatible with the
survival of a society. Today, this task is compounded enormously because we have reached the limits of the earth's carrying capacity, and knowledge acquired by science is essential
for all decisions. While analytical, left-hemisphere abilities be-

come active in the field of values, we must take care that the best of human nature does not vanish from the universe. We think of such qualities as simple intuitive human warmth, or the rare but immensely powerful experience of an interior change toward a more meaningful life. Those who experience such a change, in the words of the philosopher William Jones, "want nothing else and nothing more. They experience a new certainty, confidence, and joy."[15]

No description of human nature that leaves out such experiences is complete, and no description of a Grand Design of Nature that omits understanding of their usefulness for life on earth can become an acceptable framework for our values.

As we strive to achieve more rational attitudes, a first step is one that we might call a "transition value," because we cannot reach the desired, more rational level without it. This first step is to relax often enough and long enough from the intense striving toward personal goals to see these from a new and more distant perspective. We must learn to become aware of whom we hurt and what we destroy, lest we destroy what is most urgently needed for our survival.

For it is only the strong regard for vital qualities in human nature, such as a sense of fairness and integrity, that will give us the right and the power to stand up against the debasement and destruction of mankind and of our earth.

Widening the Focus on Religion

With the ever growing impact of science on our lives religion and spirituality have a greater role to play in reminding us of our humanity. There is no contradiction between the two. Each gives us valuable insights into the other. Both science and spirituality tell us of the fundamental unity of all things. This understanding is crucial if we are to take positive and decisive action on the pressing global concern with the environment.
—The Dalai Lama

We need models [of reality] for an orientation that ultimately coincides with evolution. —Herbert V. Guenther

So far we have confined ourselves to both the religions and the science of the West. Why? For one thing, the conflict between science and religion has emerged most sharply in Western culture, in part because modern science arose in the West and reached its greatest heights there. Secondly, Western culture, including Western science, has spread around the entire globe in the last few centuries. That influence has even accelerated in the years since World War II, when the tide of direct political control—the colonial empires—ebbed. Ideas take root more firmly than colonial regimes.

It is now time to widen our focus on religion and draw attention to belief systems, both modern and ancient, that already express reverence for evolving nature and therefore might be especially open to Sperry's thinking.

One of these is process theology, based on Albert North Whitehead's process philosophy and his belief that reality is best perceived in terms of *event-thinking* rather than *substance-thinking*. In other words, relationships between substances and their dynamic nature are of first importance rather than the substances themselves, which are but special instances of these relationships. That point of view has been lucidly described by the Australian biologist Charles Birch (who received the 1989 Templeton Prize—the highest prize in religion—for his attempts to establish a new ecological ethic) and John B. Cobb, Jr., the foremost American process theologist, in their book *The Liberation of Life*.[16]

Another is Buddhism, which shares with Sperry's philosophy not only a profound awe for the grandeur and beauty of nature, but also a sincere regard for the holistic thinking methods of the right hemisphere—thinking methods that Sperry's research has solidly anchored to a scientific understanding of human nature (and thus made less destructible). While these are characteristics also of other Eastern religions, Buddhism—especially its most advanced school, Mahayana Buddhism, which is distinctive through its open-mindedness—shares with Sperry (and with science) a great respect for the value of criticism. Unquestioned acceptance of the views of other persons, even if transmitted through tradition, is discouraged.

According to the philosopher of science and teacher of Buddhism Jeremy Hayward, critical thought, meditation, and action form an indivisible unit. "First, one analyzes one's world, self and perceptual process in order to eradicate wrong views of reality; then one practices meditation in order to allow the correct view derived from analysis to permeate to the deeper levels of one's mind/body; finally, because of such permeation, one's speech and action are in accord with this view."[17]

Meditation means for the Mahayana Buddhist a cleansing of the mind of all preconceived thoughts and concepts, opening it for direct experience of the "nonduality" of self and universe. After years of disciplined practice of meditation it is possible to attain the deepest insights human nature is capable of, together with the conviction that the ultimate truth has been reached—the truth that lies beyond the veil of everyday knowledge. A powerful inner transformation occurs that cannot be described in words and that is known only to those who experience it: the ego is being transcended and one realizes that no separate "things" exist, apart from ever changing dynamic patterns which, together with our perceptions, cocreate the world that we call "real." True reality is without boundaries.[18]

It is astonishing how liberating that truth can be. "We discover that the 'belief context' proposed by Buddhists turns out to be freedom, at a profound level, from all systems of belief."[19]

Such discoveries are not confined to persons who, like the author of the above quotation, were first and foremost educated in the West. The Dalai Lama, for instance, upon receiving the Nobel Peace Prize in Oslo in 1989, declared that though religion and spirituality are closely tied to our humanity, a sense of empathy and responsibility for our common fate (including that of our biosphere) can be developed "with or without religion."[20] This remarkable man, who has been intensely trained in the ways of Buddhism since early infancy, who spends half of each day in meditation, and who should, according to Buddhist be-

lief, therefore have prime access to fundamental truth, is prepared to go even further. "Should reincarnation be scientifically
disproved," he says, "we will have to accept that. The scrip-
tures will be revised."[21]

Such is the power of openness. The Dalai Lama does not reject science. He is not afraid that it will destroy his religion. He
sees his religion as strong enough to incorporate science and to
neutralize its dangerous and inhuman aspects. He knows that
science is a tool that will help to lead compassion into active
service against suffering on earth. For the Dalai Lama, it is not
Buddhism that must be saved. It is humanity. It is our earth.

Any religion able to encourage such thinking—whether of
the West or the East—deserves our greatest respect.

And here, for the first time, religion is now met by a science
also open to fundamental new insights, a science that acknowledges that reality cannot be accurately described while leaving
out subjective experience and the power of values that affect the
workings of our brains, guide our actions, and determine our
future.

The result is a world with room for the contributions of both
science and religion, the left hemisphere and the right—a world
beyond the present world divided.

·10·
Beyond
a World Divided

In the face of the magnitude of our problems, we are in deep need of recognizing extraordinary human beings.
—Jonas Salk

What has gone before has dwelt on the ideas and accomplishments of a single person, yet our allegiance is to our species and to our earth; and from that vantage point the significance of Roger Sperry's philosophy becomes apparent. We must consider the larger context in which his thoughts will be expressed and, perhaps, applied; the problem of integrating his theories into current thinking, inside science and without; and the long-range consequences of those theories. In human society as well as in other parts of nature, the same elements may be beneficial in one constellation, lethal in another.

Water, for instance, can bring life to a creature dying of thirst in the desert, but death to a drowning being struggling for air. Policies, transplanted from a climate of trust and concern into one of mistrust and hatred, may likewise reverse their effects.

The right approach is always crucial. For instance, neither indifference nor accusations are likely to solve the overpopulation problem; but genuine concern, like that attributed to Martin Luther King, Jr., has a good chance of leading to lasting change.

Unlike plagues of the dark ages or contemporary diseases we do not yet understand, the modern plague of overpopulation is soluble by means we have discovered and with resources we possess. What is lacking is not sufficient knowledge of the solution but universal consciousness of the gravity of the problem and education of the billions who are its victims.[1]

That is the language that will bring about results.

Once we grasp this fact and all its implications, we cannot advocate even the most promising thoughts without thinking simultaneously of the wider context in which they will be expressed.

Such an expanded perspective will not detract from the appreciation of Sperry's work: quite the contrary. The significance of any person's life-work, whether scientific, literary, or in the realm of public affairs, is judged at least partly on its capacity to contribute to a larger whole, *and on the quality of that resulting whole.*

Progress by integrating highly selective elements is a fundamental characteristic of evolution. The brain, for example, perceives reality using a two-step process. First, from billions of impressions crowding in through the senses, the neurons of the brain select those that are most relevant, enhancing their strength, while tuning out (or at least "turning down") competing impressions. Only a few events in the outside world trigger our senses; of these, far fewer still reach the higher levels of the brain. And so the screening process continues until the information arriving at the final "association centers" in the brain—where sensory inputs are integrated and put to use in decision making—has only the most marginal resemblance to the "real world." What is transmitted is not reality itself but those aspects of it that matter in an individual's life. To accomplish that feat, the brain employs great numbers of amplifiers, inhibitors, feedback loops, and the like.[2] Without such screening, or *coding,* we would be unable to make sense of the world: our minds would be utterly blank. We perceive only what stands out.

For thought to occur, though, a second step is required; innumerable single perceptions are combined into a new whole: conscious thought. It is that new creation, that new whole, that adds to each contributing perception a special significance.

Similarly, the life of our society, of humanity, of the biosphere, depends upon both steps: the *recognition* of extraordinary human beings, and the *integration* of their work into a superhuman body of wisdom.

Yet, though all their contributions would pass into oblivion with the death of our civilization, those who have risen to the zenith through unending competitive striving cannot at the moment of success change their attitudes. Nor can we hardly expect them to do so. Cooperation depends upon compatibility. How can a pioneering genius, exhilarated by his discoveries of new worlds of thought, view cooperation as other than degrading? And, too, cooperation depends upon complementarity. How can someone whose advance beyond even the best has been the result of dedicating all his being toward the achievement of *one* aim even perceive the merits of other ways of thought?[3]

To step forward in the history of human thinking, a person has to estimate his own contribution as large enough to deserve the superhuman efforts needed for its success; the strain and torture involved in pioneer labor cannot otherwise be sustained. That need, however, results in the solid "locking-in" of a combat-mentality, just at the stage where integration and cooperation would lead to even greater progress.

But there is a solution, and nature—blind, uncaring, prehuman nature—has already found it.

In *Chance and Necessity,* Jacques Monod described allosteric enzymes and their unique capacity to bind to two or more entities with differing structural or chemical affinities, enabling them to cooperate for the benefit of the entire cell in spite of their incompatibility with one another. As a result, the health and viability of the cell as a whole are enhanced.

Who or what are mankind's counterparts of the cell's allosteric enzymes?

They are individuals who understand the benefit to our society and our earth of two or more incompatible independent persons of great merit, and who can interpret and integrate the thinking of each, putting that integrated whole to work in leading mankind ahead.

The well-known German ethologist Konrad Lorenz has described how this might work in practice.

> The significance of genuinely new, epoch-making discoveries, especially in the natural sciences, is almost invariably overrated at the beginning, and by the discoverer himself more than anyone else. It is the prerogative of the genius who has found a new explanatory principle to over-assess its scope. Jacques Loeb thought he could explain all animal and human behavior in terms of the principle of tropism; Pavlov thought he could do so on the basis of the conditioned reflex, while Freud was guilty of some comparable errors. . . . Even within the confines of a particular school of thought, the formation of a new common view begins with someone departing from what had hitherto been accepted, but overstating his case. His colleagues, or more desirably his pupils, less inspired but with greater powers of analysis, then have the task of damping down the excessive oscillation and arresting the movement at the proper point. The reverse process can actually hinder the advancement of knowledge by establishing a dogma.[4]

Leon Kass, professor at the University of Chicago and writer in the field of philosophy of biology, also recognizes that new knowledge, if advocated as "supreme," will arrest progress. He warns that "the last thing we need are prejudgments or ideologies . . . that usurp the place of genuine thought."[5]

Competition, for instance, has long been heralded as *the* motor of progress in physical and mental evolution, as *the* essential element in raising the "quality of life," while cooperation and altruism have been derided as leading to stagnation and degradation. That picture is changing.

As the great panorama of the ascendance of life is displayed in our minds, we recognize that the most significant advances

have occurred not through competition, but through cooperation. Elementary particles, atoms, molecules, living cells, multicellular organisms, societies—all these tell stories of magnificent forward thrusts in evolution made possible by the
discovery of compatible constellations among differing forces.
Our own brains, our own experiences of being free and proud
and powerful, are themselves the result of precise and minutely
organized interactions of billions of cells, of trillions of atoms
and molecules. Cooperation, as much as competition, has
brought us to where we are; but emphasis on cooperation is
needed to bring us farther.

Similarly, altruism, the intuitive knowledge that the feelings
and longings of other persons, even those unknown to us, are
similar to our own—that hidden miracles exist in the human
soul—cannot possibly be degrading if the consequences of our
actions are carefully considered. Humanity cannot progress by
discarding our consciences, as some recommend. The opposite
is needed: the *extension* of our consciences to include concern
for the fate of future generations, the fate of our biosphere.

To *discard* our consciences would lower the worth of humanity itself. Mutual disrespect would become pervasive enough to
suggest that eradicating the human species from the face of the
earth would be a blessing for the further evolution of life—a
point of view already expressed by many scholars and observ-
ers of the human condition.[6]

We believe that our journey ahead through the turbulence of
unforeseen events will succeed best if guided by the understanding that our consciences, our species, and our biosphere
form an indivisible unit.

Those who argue that overpopulation, which lies at the core
of all our other problems, could solve itself if we would just get
rid of our consciences and get on with "what has to be done"—
whether it be infanticide, triage, genocide, or other unthinkable
final solutions—should contemplate one of the most thoughtful
questions Sperry has ever raised: "What form religion and the
teachings of Christ, Muhammed, Buddha, Confucius, and other

founders might have taken, if Copernicus, Darwin, Einstein, and all the rest had come before their time instead of after?"[7]

Every one of the founders of great religions would have taught differently, had they been enlightened by the new knowledge. They would have taught us to feel responsible for the long-range effects of all our actions. They would *not* have taught us to discard our consciences. They would have known that the same aim, the survival of our species, can be approached either with reverence for the unknown treasures of the human mind, or with blind destructiveness of the best in humanity. The first approach will bring us success through reason, insight, and long-range concerns. The second approach will lead only to failure and disgust with our species—a long winter of the soul with no prospect of a spring.

Those who have argued that the demise of humankind would be a blessing to our earth should be reminded that all the beauty of nature we experience, all the meaningfulness and grandeur of the universe, is created by the interaction of our nervous systems with that universe—and would vanish as our brains reverted to dust. It might be millions or even hundreds of millions of years before intelligent beings would arise again, this time, one hopes, not to make the same mistakes. And it might be never. Clearly, rather than hoping for destruction and the cleaning of the slate, we would be better developing the wisdom of our own species, encouraging pioneers seeking to expand that wisdom—so long as openness toward new knowledge remains part of our greatest good.

Nor is neglecting our own biosphere and transferring to another suitable planet a viable option. The other worlds of the solar system are hostile and could provide homes for man only through use of technology of the highest sophistication. They will challenge our children but they are no substitute for earth; and the pictures returned by our space probes ignite a profound appreciation of conditions on our own globe and a deep love of our home planet. Astronauts gazing back at the earth, floating in space, reported feeling the same emotions.[8]

A search for contributors to a body of wisdom involving our destiny has taught me that the most mature and responsible persons are those who do not distinguish the fate of humanity from the fate of our earth.[9]

Reflections

Human survival depends upon the mutual illumination of facts and values. Psychology and the behavioral sciences have already undergone a paradigm shift from a fifty-year-long rejection of consciousness, ending in the mid-sixties, to the current enormous interest in the phenomenon. We hope that a large number of the world's scientists, as well as followers of the great religions, will also recognize the danger of a world divided by two contrasting systems of belief.

And so we looked first at Sperry's philosophy from the perspective of science. The study of the brain, if it disregards consciousness and values, leaves us blind to its most spectacular capacities; in fact, it distorts reality. Then, examining his work from a different vantage point, that of religion, we concluded that the pursuit of values while disregarding facts is futile and cruel.

The hour is late, the problems confronting us immense, and inhumane, catastrophic solutions become ever more likely the longer we delay. Our only hope lies in replacing a laissez-faire mentality with a willingness to shoulder responsibility for the future.

Assuming such responsibility, vast though it is, does not eliminate joy. Joy becomes less superficial, however, and gains in depth and content. The knowledge that we are copartners of evolving nature, whether intentionally and consciously or not, can lead to emotional experiences of the most profound kind.

The grand scheme of evolving nature has been and will be interpreted in many different ways. When Sperry suggests that we accept its manifest forward and upward thrust as our high-

est value and guiding principle, he understands and interprets
it as a progression

from misinformation to true knowledge

from incompatible worldviews to a unifying belief system

from catastrophic disasters and cruelty to humane solutions to our global predicament

from a hands-off policy in the face of foreseeable epidemics
and global mass starvation to an attitude of foresight,
concern, and responsibility

from mutual destruction in the name of incompatible absolute truths to an empirical framework for values

from a narrow egocentric and anthropocentric perspective
to a larger vision, including not only all mankind, present and future, but the entire interrelated web of life

from a blind rush toward extinction to an enlightened advance toward yet unrevealed further wonders of evolution

Epilogue

And now, in the end, I should be less abstract and say something concrete about the person whose philosophy I have discussed. This is difficult for me. If I think about him in concrete terms at all—and this is rare because the significance of his work for our future predominates—I see a lover of solitude, of nature, of beauty, of poetry. I see a striver for excellence, incessantly dissatisfied with himself and with others. I see everything he touches, even the products of his spare time, turn into masterpieces. The sculptures he made turn his home into a museum of exquisite taste. His interest in fossils led to his discovery of one of the largest ammonites in the world, now mounted at one end of his living room. But he is not easy to live with, and his wonderful wife has been called a saint.

I see a perfectionist, a disciplined laborer, improving his own writing through innumerable revisions and demanding the utmost of himself with an obsession bordering on cruelty. But he does not work constantly; his "anti-brain-strain activities" (his own expression)—carefully scheduled to achieve top performance during working hours—include relaxed evenings at home and weeks of fishing, swimming, or exploring the remote and barren shorelines of the Baja, a rocky Mexican peninsula jutting into the Pacific.

If an urgent task demands it, however, he is a tremendous worker. At the age of seventy-two, ravaged by his slowly progressing paralysis, he rewrote a long and difficult paper—a work I estimated would take several months—within a single week, *although he had to undergo an eye operation during that same week.*

The three words describing his nature most accurately would be *courage, willpower,* and *self-discipline.* Most of all, I see him as a fighter—drawn by difficulties, conquering obstacles anyone else would judge undefeatable.

This is the man who has set himself the task of turning the world of Arnold's "Dover Beach"—the world with "neither joy nor love nor light"—into a much more real one, a world in which joy and love and light are part of the reality of scientists as well as of the religious; a world in which we may hope again, like the pioneers of the Enlightenment, that the "clash of ignorant armies at night" may be ended in the coming of a new dawn.

But how can Sperry's point of view be integrated into the solid, broader framework of human knowledge? How can the merging of science and values become a self-evident part of the majority's mind-set?

Someone who worked closely with Sperry for over thirty years once said: "Dr. Sperry is such a genius; if he just knew how to acknowledge the work of others, the world would lie at his feet."

Another person, himself one of the greatest scientists I know, seemed to have more insight. "I can understand him," he said of Sperry; "his thoughts are too valuable, his time is too valuable. He cannot be expected to penetrate into the minds of others and even less to adjust the expression of his own ideas to the framework of their conceptions. We have to do that for him."

Echoes from these two conversations follow me everywhere: "The world would lie at his feet" and "We have to do that for him."

—*Erika Erdmann*

Appendix:
Roger Sperry's Key Papers

The Development of the Brain

Sperry, Roger. "The Problem of Central Nervous Reorganization After Nerve Regeneration and Muscle Transposition." *Quarterly Review of Biology* 20 (December, 1945): 311–69.

———. "Regulative Factors in the Orderly Growth of Neural Circuits." *Growth Symposium* 10 (1951): 63–87.

———. "Chemoaffinity in the Orderly Growth of Nerve Fiber Patterns and Connections." *Proceedings of the National Academy of Science of the United States of America* 50 (October, 1963): 703–10.

The Split Brain

Sperry, Roger. "Cerebral Organization and Behavior." *Science* 133 (June, 1961): 1749–57.

Sperry, Roger, M. S. Gazzaniga, and J. E. Bogen. "Interhemispheric Relationships: The Neocortical Commisures; Syndromes of Hemispheric Disconnection." *Handbook of Clinical Neurology* 4 (1969): 273–90.

Sperry, Roger. "Lateral Specialization in the Surgically Separated Hemispheres." *Neurosciences Third Study Program*, edited by F. Schmitt and F. Worden, vol. 3, pp. 5–19. Cambridge: MIT Press, 1974.

———. "Consciousness, Personal Identity, and the Divided Brain." Doubleday Lecture, Smithsonian Institution, Washington, D.C. In *Two Hemispheres—One Brain: Functions of the Corpus Callosum*, edited by M. Ptito and H. Jasper, pp. 3–20. New York: Alan R. Liss, 1986.

Consciousness and Values

Sperry, Roger. "Mind, Brain and Humanist Values." In *New Views of the Nature of Man*, ed. J. R. Platt, pp. 71–92. Chicago: University of Chicago Press, 1965. Reprinted (condensed) in *Bulletin of Atomic Scientists* 12, no. 7 (September 22, 1966): 2–6.

─────. "A Modified Concept of Consciousness." *Psychological Review* 76 (November, 1969): 532–36. Reprinted in *Theories in Contemporary Psychology*, edited by M. H. Marx and F. E. Gradson, pp. 451–57. New York: Macmillan, 1976.

─────. "Science and the Problem of Values." *Perspectives in Biology and Medicine* 16 (Autumn 1972): 115–30. Reprinted in *Zygon* 9 (1974): 7–21.

─────. "Changing Priorities." *Annual Review of Neuroscience* 4 (1981): 1–15.

─────. "Structure and Significance of the Consciousness Revolution." *Journal of Mind and Behavior* 8 (Winter, 1987): 37–65.

─────. "Psychology's Mentalist Paradigm and the Religion/Science Tension." *American Psychologist* 43 (1988): 607–13.

Sperry's major papers on values written up to 1983 have been collected in Roger Sperry, *Science and Moral Priority: Merging Mind, Brain and Human Values*, ed. Ruth Anshen (New York: Columbia University Press, 1983; New York: Praeger, 1985).

His major papers on consciousness, together with his later papers on values, will be published in a forthcoming book.

A list of 157 papers written by Sperry in the fields mentioned above is available from his office. In addition, innumerable papers written by his students and coworkers, as well as by other scientists pursuing his research in all parts of the world, can be found in journals and textbooks on the mind-brain relation.

A collection of some of the key papers by Sperry's students will be found in: Colwyn Trevarthen, ed., *Brain Circuits and Functions of the Mind: Essays in Honor of Roger W. Sperry* (New York: Cambridge University Press, 1990).

Epigraph Sources

Chapter 1. *The Rift*

Snow, C. P. *Public Affairs*. New York: Scribner, 1971.

Chapter 2. *A World Divided*

Monod, Jacques. *Chance and Necessity*. New York: Knopf, 1971.

Part 2. *The Quest*

Jones, William T. *The Sciences and the Humanities*. Berkeley and Los Angeles: University of California Press, 1965.

Sperry, Roger, "Changing Priorities," *Annual Review of Neuroscience* 4 (1981): 1–15.

Wordsworth, William. Quoted in Roger Sperry's *Science and Moral Priority*. New York: Columbia University Press, 1983; New York: Praeger, 1985.

Chapter 3. *The Lure of the Mind-Brain Problem*

Sperry, Roger. "Neurology and the Mind-Brain Problem." *American Scientist* 40 (1952): 291–312.

Chapter 4. *Concern with Consciousness*

Weisskopf, Victor. *Knowledge and Wonder*. Garden City, N.Y.: Doubleday, 1962.

Chapter 5. *Concern with Values*

Sperry, Roger. "Bridging Science and Values." *American Psychologist* 32 (1977): 237–45.

EPIGRAPH SOURCES

Chapter 6. Reception of a Paradigm

Kuhn, Thomas. *The Structure of Scientific Revolutions*. Chicago: The University of Chicago Press, 1970.

Pope, Alexander. *An Essay on Man*. Frank Brady, ed. New York: Bobbs-Merrill, 1965.

Chapter 7. In Search of Reference Points

Sperry, Roger. "Changing Priorities." (1981). (The quote used here is from a reprint of the paper in *Science and Moral Priority*.)

Snow, C. P. *Public Affairs*, 1971.

Salk, Jonas. Personal communication, 13 January 1985. Dr. Salk's permission to use this quote is gratefully acknowledged.

Part 3. The Hope

Kass, Leon. "Modern Science and Ethics." *University of Chicago Magazine* (Summer 1984).

Morgan, C. Lloyd. *Emergent Evolution*. London: Williams and Norgate, 1923.

Chapter 8. Toward Left-Hemisphere Acceptance

Jones, William T. *The Sciences and the Humanities*, 1965.

Skinner, B. F. "Behaviorism at 50," in *Behaviorism and Phenomenology*. Edited by T. W. Wann. Chicago: University of Chicago Press, 1964.

Harman, Willis. *Global Mind Change*. Indianapolis, Ind.: Knowledge Systems, 1988.

Chapter 9. Toward Right-Hemisphere Acceptance

Boulding, Kenneth. *Ecodynamics*. Beverly Hills: Sage Publications, 1978.

Thomas, Lewis. *The Youngest Science*. New York: Viking Press, 1983.

Gyatso, Tenzin, the 14th Dalai Lama. "Address by His Holiness the Dalai Lama on the Occasion of the Acceptance of the Alfred P. Nobel Prize for Peace, Oslo, Oct. 10, 1989." Stockholm: The Nobel Foundation, 1989.

Guenther, Herbert. *From Reductionism to Creativity*. Boston: Shambhala, 1989.

Chapter 10. Beyond a World Divided

Salk, Jonas. *Anatomy of Reality*. New York: Columbia University Press, 1983. Reprinted by New York: Praeger Publishers (now Greenwood), 1984.

Notes

Chapter 1. The Rift

1. Francis Schaeffer, *A Christian Manifesto* (Westchester, Ill.: Crossway Books, 1981), p. 73.
2. Burnham Beckwith, *Religion, Philosophy and Science* (New York: Philosophical Library, 1957), p. 203.
3. Ibid., p. 195.
4. Ibid., p. 227.
5. Schaeffer, *Christian Manifesto,* p. 21.
6. Arnold Toynbee and Daisaku Ikeda, *Choose Life* (London: Oxford University Press, 1979), p. 214.
7. Norman Cousins, "Norman Cousins, a Spokesman for the Human Race," *The Mother Earth News* 90 (November–December 1984).
8. Albert Einstein (1917), as quoted in Timothy Ferris, "The Other Einstein," *Science* 83 (October 1983).

Chapter 2. A World Divided

1. Jacques Monod, *Chance and Necessity* (New York: Knopf, 1971).
2. Arthur Peacocke, *Intimations of Reality: Critical Realism in Science and Religion,* Menden Hall Lectures (Notre Dame, Ind.: University of Notre Dame Press, 1984), p. 35.
3. Aaron Kupperman, "Cosmology—The Origin of Life, Evolution, and Religion," lecture at the California Institute of Technology, 12 February 1987.
4. Werner Heisenberg, *Physics and Beyond* (New York: Harper & Row, 1971).
5. Friedrich Hayek, *The Sensory Order* (Chicago: University of Chicago Press, 1952).

6. John Eccles, "The Importance of Brain Research for the Educational, Cultural, and Scientific Future of Mankind," *Perspectives of Biology and Medicine* 12 (1968/69): 61.

7. John Eccles, "Animal Consciousness and Human Self-Consciousness," in "A Tribute to W. R. Hess," *Experentia* 12 (1982): 1388.

8. John Eccles, Discussion. Proceedings of the Second International Conference on the Unity of the Sciences, Tokyo, 18–21 November 1973, in *Modern Science and Moral Values* (New York: International Cultural Foundation, 1973), p. 55.

9. Eccles, "Animal Consciousness and Human Self-Consciousness," p. 1387.

10. Eccles, Discussion in *Modern Science and Moral Values,* p. 55.

11. Eccles, "Animal Consciousness and Human Self-Consciousness," p. 1391.

12. John Eccles, *The Human Psyche,* Gifford Lectures, delivered 18 April–4 May 1979 (Berlin: Springer International, 1980), p. 69.

13. John Eccles, "Culture: the Creation of Man and the Creator of Man," in *Modern Science and Human Values,* p. 32.

14. Edward Wilson, *Sociobiology: The New Synthesis* (Cambridge, Mass.: The Belknap Press of Harvard University Press, 1975).

15. Wilson and a number of his supporters have in recent years ameliorated their degrading view of human nature and admitted that altruism, too, may have evolutionary advantages. (See, for example, Charles Lumsden and Ann Gushurst, "The Human Odyssey— Coevolution and the Mind," *Future Health* [Fall 1984].)

16. Eccles, *The Human Psyche,* p. 205.

17. Germain Grisez, *Christian Moral Principles,* vol. 1, *The Way of the Lord Jesus* (Chicago: Franciscan Herald Press, 1983), p. 105.

18. Ibid., p. 84.

19. Ibid., p. 299.

20. Francis Schaeffer, *A Christian Manifesto* (Westchester, Ill.: Crossway Books, 1981).

21. Ibid., p. 133.

22. Monod, *Chance and Necessity,* p. 171.

Part 2. Prelude: The More Encompassing Vision

1. Roger Sperry, "Changing Priorities," *Annual Review of Neuroscience* 4 (1981): 1–15.

Chapter 3. The Lure of the Mind-Brain Problem

1. Roger Sperry, "The Problem of Central Nervous Reorganization after Nerve Regeneration and Muscle Transposition," *The Quarterly Review of Biology* 20, no. 4 (1945): 311–69.
2. Roger Sperry, "Problems in the Biochemical Specifications of Neurons," in *Biochemistry of the Developing Nervous System,* ed. H. Waelch (New York: Academic Press, 1955).
3. National Science Foundation, Washington, D.C., on awarding the National Medal of Science to Roger Sperry on 18 October 1989.
4. See Viktor Hamburger, "Roger Sperry Awarded Gerard Prize," *Neuroscience Newsletter* 10, no. 4 (December 1979): 5–6; Melvin Konner, *The Tangled Wing* (New York: Holt, Rinehart & Winston, 1982); and Colwyn Trevarthen, ed., *Brain Circuits and Functions of the Mind: Essays in Honor of Roger W. Sperry* (New York: Cambridge University Press, 1990).
5. T. Adler, "Sperry Wins Science Medal," *The APA Monitor* 21, no. 3 (1990): 5–6.
6. Hamburger, "Roger Sperry Awarded Gerard Prize."
7. Ibid.
8. Roger Sperry, personal communication, April 1990. See also interview with Yvonne Baskin, *Omni* 5, no. 11 (August 1983): 71.
9. *MD* (September 1979): 51.
10. See, for example, Betty Edwards, *Drawing on the Right Side of the Brain* (Los Angeles: J. P. Tarcher, 1979).
11. Sperry has received prizes, awards, and honorary degrees too numerous to list in this short summary. In one year alone, 1979, he was presented with the Wolf Foundation Prize in Medicine by the Knesset in Jerusalem, the Ralph Gerard Prize by the American National Society for Neuroscience for "radical conceptual conversions in two different fields of inquiry," and the Albert Lasker Medical Research Award, the highest prize in American medicine, "for fundamental contributions toward knowledge of brain development and function."
12. Jacques Monod, *Chance and Necessity* (New York: Knopf, 1971).
13. John Eccles, "Brain, Speech and Consciousness," *Die Naturwissenschaften* 60 (1973): 168.
14. *Time,* 19 October 1981.

Chapter 4. Concern with Consciousness

1. Roger Sperry, personal communication, April 1990.
2. Roger Sperry, "Neurology and the Mind-Brain Problem," *American Scientist* 40 (1952): 311.
3. Jerry Fodor, "The Mind-Body Problem," *Scientific American* 244, no. 1 (1981): 114–23.
4. Later, in the 1960s, Sperry realized that this mental "interaction with the object" could "also be understood as having an actual functional role in brain processing," as he explained during a recent interview with Heidi Aspaturian of the Caltech campus newspaper. ("Roger Sperry: New Mindset on Consciousness," *On Campus* [October 1987].)
5. Roger Sperry, discussion in *The Central Nervous System and Behavior*, ed. M. A. B. Brazier (New Jersey: Madison Print, 1959), pp. 420–21.
6. Roger Sperry, "Science and the Problem of Values," *Perspectives in Biology and Medicine* 16 (1972): 116. Reprinted in *Zygon* 9 (1974).
7. *Encyclopaedia Britannica* (1986); Ernest Nagel, *The Structure of Science* (New York: Harcourt, Brace & World, 1961), p. 370; John Smart, "Physicalism and Emergence," *Neuroscience* 6 (1981): 109–13.
8. Roy Wood Sellars is most often quoted in the literature in connection with the liberation of the concept of emergence from mystical bonds, such as his book *Evolutionary Naturalism* (Chicago: The Open Court Publishing Co., 1922), and much has been written on the subject since that time. A very good recent discussion of emergence is provided by Charles Ripley ("Sperry's Concept of Consciousness," *Inquiry* 27 [1984]: 399–423), who bases it on his studies of work by Mario Bunge, such as *Treatise on Basic Philosophy*, vol. 3 (Dordrecht: Reidel, 1977).
9. Roger Sperry, "A Modified Concept of Consciousness," *Psychological Review* 76, no. 6 (1969): 533–34.
10. Roger Sperry, "Discussion: Macro versus Micro-Determinism," *Philosophy of Science* 53 (1986): 267.
11. Sperry, "A Modified Concept of Consciousness."
12. Sperry has, however, used the term *emergent causation* in several of his papers to refer to specific aspects of his philosophy, such as downward causation. For his philosophy as a whole, he has lately started to prefer the term *emergent determinism*.

13. Roger Sperry, "Problems Outstanding in the Evolution of Brain Function," James Arthur Lecture at the American Museum of Natural History in New York (1964), p. 20. Reprinted in *The Encyclopedia of Ignorance,* ed. R. Duncan and M. Weston-Smith (Oxford: Pergamon Press, 1977), pp. 423–33.

14. Roger Sperry, discussion in *The Central Nervous System and Behavior.*

15. B. F. Skinner, "Behaviorism at 50," in *Behaviorism and Phenomenology,* ed. T. W. Wann (Chicago: University of Chicago Press, 1964).

16. Dean Wooldridge, *The Machinery of the Brain* (New York: McGraw-Hill, 1963), pp. 71–72, 240.

17. John Smart, *Philosophy and Scientific Realism* (New York: Routledge and Kegan, 1963).

18. Sigmund Koch, "Psychology and Emerging Conceptions of Knowledge as Unitary," in *Behaviorism and Phenomenology,* ed. T. W. Wann, (Chicago: The University of Chicago Press, 1964), p. 32.

19. Ibid., p. 38.

20. Roger Sperry, "Mental Phenomena as Causal Determinants of Brain Function," in *Consciousness and the Brain,* ed. G. G. Globus, G. Maxwell, and I. Savodnik (New York: Plenum, 1976), p. 174. Reprinted in *Process Studies* 5 (1976): 247–56. For a demonstration of the brain's capacity to form meaningful images from the scantiest input, see Roger Sperry, "Forebrain Commissurotomy and Conscious Awareness," *Journal of Medicine and Philosophy* 2, no. 2 (1977): 106.

21. Viktor Hamburger, "Roger Sperry Awarded Gerard Prize," *Neuroscience Newsletter* 10, no. 4 (December 1979): 5–6.

22. Sperry, "The Evolution of Brain Function"; Roger Sperry, "Brain Bisection and Mechanisms of Consciousness," lecture during Study Week of the Pontificia Academia Scientarium, Rome, 28 September–4 October 1964, in *Brain and Conscious Experience,* ed. John Eccles (New York: Springer, 1966), p. 308.

23. Roger Sperry, "Mind, Brain, and Humanist Values" in *New Views of the Nature of Man,* ed. John Platt (Chicago: University of Chicago Press, 1965), pp. 71–92. Reprinted (abridged) in *Bulletin of Atomic Scientists* 12, no. 7 (1966): 2–6.

24. Thomas Kuhn, *The Structure of Scientific Revolutions* (Chicago: The University of Chicago Press, 1970), p. 24.

25. Ibid., p. 75.

26. C. P. Snow, *The Two Cultures and the Scientific Revolution* (New York: Cambridge University Press, 1959).

27. William T. Jones, *The Sciences and the Humanities* (Berkeley and Los Angeles: University of California Press, 1965), p. 11.

28. Sperry, "Mind, Brain and Humanist Values," p. 78.

29. This key paper was first addressed to the National Academy of Science and then expanded for publication.

30. Sperry, "A Modified Concept of Consciousness," p. 532.

31. John Eccles, "Conscious Experience and Memory," in *Brain and Conscious Experience,* ed. John Eccles (New York: Springer, 1966), p. 248.

32. Roger Sperry, "Mind-Brain Interaction: Mentalism, Yes; Dualism, No," *Neuroscience* 5 (1980): 195–206.

33. Karl Popper and John Eccles, *The Self and Its Brain* (New York: Springer, 1977). See also John Eccles, "Brain, Speech and Consciousness," *Die Naturwissenschaften* 60 (1973): 167–76; and John Eccles, Preface to *Critique of the Psycho-Physical Identity Theory* by E. P. Polten (The Hague: Mouton, 1973). (Eccles's synapse-theory is described in *The Neurophysiological Basis of Mind* (Oxford: Clarendon Press, 1953).

34. Popper and Eccles, *The Self and Its Brain.*

35. Roger Sperry, "Structure and Significance of the Consciousness Revolution," *The Journal of Mind and Behavior* 8, no. 1 (1987): 37–65.

36. Roger Sperry, "Bridging Science and Values: A Unifying View of Mind and Brain," *American Psychologist* 32 (1977): 240. Reprinted in *Zygon* 14 (1979).

37. Sperry's key paper "Mind, Brain, and Humanist Values" (1965) has been condensed in the *Bulletin of Atomic Scientists* 12, no. 7 (1966): 2–6.

38. Roger Sperry, "An Objective Approach to Subjective Experience: Further Explanation of a Hypothesis," *Psychological Review* 77 (1970): 585–90; Dalbir Bindra, "The Problem of Subjective Experience: Puzzlement on Reading R. W. Sperry's 'A Modified Concept of Consciousness,' " *Psychological Review* 77 (1970): 581–84.

39. Sperry, "An Objective Approach to Subjective Experience," p. 586.

40. Ibid.

41. Ibid., p. 587.

42. Ibid.
43. Ibid., p. 588.
44. Ibid., p. 589.
45. Roger Sperry, interview with Yvonne Baskin, *Omni* 5, no. 11 (1983): 98.

Chapter 5. Concern with Values

1. Roger Sperry, "Psychology's Mentalist Paradigm and the Religion/Science Tension," *American Psychologist* 43 (1988): 611.
2. Ibid.
3. Roger Sperry, "Science and the Problem of Values," *Perspectives in Biology and Medicine* 16 (1972): 127, 128. Reprinted in *Zygon* 9 (1974): 7–21.
4. Sperry, "Psychology's Mentalist Paradigm," p. 612.
5. Roger Sperry, "Changing Priorities," *Annual Review of Neuroscience* 4 (1981): 9.
6. Ibid.
7. Roger Sperry, "Neurology and the Mind-Brain Problem," *American Scientist* 40 (1952): 311.
8. Roger Sperry, *Science and Moral Priority* (New York: Columbia University Press, 1983), p. 4. (Reprinted New York: Praeger [now Greenwood Press], 1985.)
9. Roger Sperry, "Changed Concepts of Brain and Consciousness: Some Value Implications," lecture as part of the 1982/83 Isthmus Foundation Lectures in Science and Religion, in The Perkins School of Theology's *Perkins Journal* 36, no. 4 (1983): 21–32. Reprinted in *Zygon* 20 (1985): 56.
10. Sperry, "Science and the Problem of Values," pp. 124–25.
11. Ibid., p. 115.
12. Ibid., p. 117.
13. Roger Sperry, "Changing Priorities," *Annual Review of Neuroscience* 4 (1981): 7.
14. Sperry, "Science and the Problem of Values," p. 129.
15. Roger Sperry, "Bridging Science and Values: A Unifying View of Mind and Brain," *American Psychologist* 32 (1977): 237–45.
16. Garrett Hardin, "An Ecolate View of the Human Predicament," *Alternatives* 7 (1981): 249, quoting from D. R. Klein, "The Introduction, Increase and Crash of Reindeer on St. Matthew Island," *Journal of Wildlife Management* 32 (1968): 350–57.

17. Sperry, "Changing Priorities."
18. Roger Sperry, "Problems Outstanding in the Evolution of Brain Function," James Arthur Lecture at the American Museum of Natural History in New York, 1964. Reprinted in *The Encyclopaedia of Ignorance*, ed. R. Duncan and M. Weston-Smith (Oxford: Pergamon Press, 1977), pp. 423–33.
19. Roger Sperry, "Mind, Brain and Humanist Values," in *New Views of the Nature of Man*, ed. John Platt (Chicago: University of Chicago Press, 1965), p. 72. Condensed in *Bulletin of Atomic Scientists* 12, no. 7 (Sept. 22, 1966): 2–6.
20. Sperry, "Psychology's Mentalist Paradigm," p. 612.
21. Sperry, "The Problem of Values," p. 121.
22. Ibid., p. 128.
23. Karl Popper, "Conversation with Karl Popper," in *Modern British Philosophy*, ed. Bryan Magee (Oxford: Oxford University Press, 1986), pp. 96–97.
24. Nicholas Maxwell, "Articulating the Aims of Science," *Nature* 265 (6 January 1977).
25. Sperry, "Changing Priorities," p. 8.
26. William T. Jones, *The Sciences and the Humanities* (Berkeley and Los Angeles: University of California Press, 1965).
27. Sperry, "Problems Outstanding in the Evolution of Brain Function," p. 20.
28. Ibid., p. 21. The subject is discussed in most of Sperry's papers on values; see, for example, his "Psychology's Mentalist Paradigm," p. 610.

Chapter 6. Reception of a Paradigm

1. M. E. Grenander, "The Mind Is Its Own Place," *Methodology and Science* 16, no. 3 (1983).
2. Thomas Kuhn, *The Structure of Scientific Revolutions* (Chicago: The University of Chicago Press, 1970), p. 84–85.
3. Stuart Sutherland, "Thoughts of Sorts" [Review of Sperry's *Science and Moral Priority*], *Nature* 302 (28 April 1983): 774.
4. Max Delbrueck, "Max Delbrueck," oral history from interviews, second installment, *Engineering and Science* 43 (May-June 1980): 21–27.
5. Roger Sperry, "Bridging Science and Values: A Unifying View of Mind and Brain," *American Psychologist* 32 (1977): 240.

6. W. N. Dember, "Motivation and the Cognitive Revolution," *American Psychologist* 29 (1974): 161–68.
7. Michael Polanyi, *The Tacit Dimension* (New York: Doubleday, 1966), p. 47.
8. Blaise Pascal, *Pensées* (1670). Reprinted (Everyman Editions, 1931), p. 235.
9. Roger Sperry, "Science and the Problem of Values," *Perspectives in Biology and Medicine* 16 (1972): 115–30. Reprinted in *Zygon* 9 (1974): 7–21. Reprinted in *Science and Moral Priority* (1983, 1985), pp. 22, 23.
10. Roger Sperry, "Psychology's Mentalist Paradigm and the Religion/Science Tension," *American Psychologist* 43 (1988): 611.
11. See, for example, *Peace and World Order Studies: A Curriculum Guide* (New York: New York World Policy Institute, 1984).
12. Robert M. Pirsig defends in his book *Zen and the Art of Motorcycle Maintenance: An Inquiry into Values* (New York: Morrow, 1974) passionately and dramatically his conviction that the term "quality" *cannot* be defined.
13. Lewis Mumford, *The Transformations of Man* (New York: Harper & Brothers, 1956).
14. Ervin Laszlo, *The Inner Limits of Mankind* (Elmsford, N.J.: Pergamon Press, 1978).
15. Charles B. Birch and John Cobb, Jr., *The Liberation of Life* (New York: Cambridge University Press, 1981), p. 236.

Chapter 7. In Search of Reference Points

1. Roy L. Walford, *Maximum Lifespan* (Toronto: George J. McLeod, 1983), p. 189.
2. Leon Kass, "Modern Science and Ethics," *University of Chicago Magazine* (Summer 1984).
3. Roger Sperry, "Changing Priorities," *Annual Review of Neuroscience* 4 (1981): 3.
4. Ibid., pp. 7–8.
5. Ibid., p. 8; Roger Sperry, "Response to Critique of Howard Slaatte," *Contemporary Philosophy* 10, no. 10 (1985): 3–4.
6. Jonas Salk, *Survival of the Wisest* (New York: Harper & Row, 1973), p. 77.
7. Ernst Gombrich, "Bicentennial Address: Focus on the Arts and

Humanities," *Bulletin of the American Academy of Arts and Sciences* 35, no. 4 (1982): 22.

8. Roger Sperry, "Science and the Problem of Values," *Perspectives in Biology and Medicine* 16 (1972): 127. Reprinted in *Zygon* 9 (1974): 7–21.

9. Ibid.

10. *New York Times Book Review,* 27 March 1983, sec. 7: 18, 20.

11. M. E. Grenander, "The Mind Is Its Own Place," *Methodology and Science* 16, no.3 (1983).

12. Arthur Peacocke, who lectures extensively throughout the world on the need to bridge the science-religion chasm, has also (like Burhoe) received the Templeton Prize for Progress in Religion.

13. Arthur Peacocke, *Creation and the World of Science*, The Bampton Lectures, 1978 (Oxford: Clarendon Press, 1979), p. 127.

14. Thomas Natsoulas, Charles Ripley, and Howard Slaatte are some of the persons interpreting Sperry's mind-brain theory as compatible with materialism; Peacocke and William Uttal also see no problem with a materialistic interpretation of the mind, *if* matter is understood in the most advanced sense, that is, as a dynamic rather than static phenomenon.

15. William Uttal, *The Psychobiology of Mind* (Hillsdale, N.J.: Erlbaum, 1978), p. 14.

16. Roger Sperry, "Mind-Brain Interaction: Mentalism, Yes; Dualism, No," *Neuroscience* 5 (1980): 202–203.

17. Peacocke, *Creation and the World of Science*, p. 128.

18. William Wimsatt, "Reductionism, Levels of Organization, and the Mind-Body Problem," in *Consciousness and the Brain*, ed. G. G. Globus, G. Maxwell, and I. Savodnik, (New York: Plenum, 1976), p. 205.

19. Ibid., editor's comment, p. 199.

20. Mario Bunge, *Treatise on Basic Philosophy*, vol. 3 (Dordrecht: Reidel, 1977).

21. *Choice* 20 (June 1983): 1532.

22. Stuart Sutherland, "Thoughts of Sorts", *Nature* 302 (28 April 1983): 774.

23. George Gaylord Simpson, *This View of Life* (New York: Harcourt, Brace & World, 1964).

24. Paul Weiss, "Toward Unity of Culture: A Program for a Program," *Zygon* 2 (1967): 223–30.

25. George Pugh, *The Biological Origin of Human Values* (New York: Basic Books, 1977).

Chapter 8. Toward Left-Hemisphere Acceptance

1. Roger Sperry, "Discussion: Macro- Versus Micro-Determinism," *Philosophy of Science* 53 (1986): 265–70. (Response to R. L. Klee's "Micro-Determinism and Concepts of Emergence.")

2. Ibid., p. 266.

3. R. L. Klee, "Micro-Determinism and Concepts of Emergence," *Philosophy of Science* 51 (1984): 44–63.

4. Referee's Report no. 850W, *Philosophy of Science*, official journal of the Philosophy of Science Association.

5. Roger Sperry, interview with Yvonne Baskin, *Omni* 5, no. 11 (1983): 75.

6. Ibid.

7. Both William Wimsatt and E. M. Dewan presented their papers immediately following Sperry's speech "Mental Phenomena as Causal Determinants of Brain Function" at the conference Dialogues on Brain and Consciousness at the University of California at Irvine during April 1973. At that date, Sperry's key paper on the mind-brain problem, "A Modified Concept of Consciousness" (1969), had had enough time to elicit thoughtful and well-considered responses. Both Dewan's and Wimsatt's papers are thoroughly worked-out contributions in support of Sperry's point of view. Although the intent of the conference had been to discuss process philosophy, the three papers in succession drew a disproportionate amount of attention toward the theory of emergent causation. (Ref. G. G. Globus, G. Maxwell and I. Savodnik, eds., *Consciousness and the Brain* [New York: Plenum, 1976]).

8. Edmond M. Dewan, "Consciousness as an Emergent Causal Agent in the Context of Control System Theory," in Globus et al., *Consciousness and the Brain*, p. 182.

9. Ibid.

10. Ibid., p. 192.

11. Ibid., p. 193.

12. William Wimsatt, "Reductionism, Levels of Organization, and the Mind-Body Problem," in *Consciousness and the Brain*, ed. Globus, pp. 199–267.

13. Roger Sperry, "Neurology and the Mind-Brain Problem," *American Scientist* 40 (1952): 295.

14. Roger Sperry, "Brain Bisection and Mechanisms of Consciousness," lecture during Study Week of the Pontificia Academia Scientarium, Rome, 28 September–4 October 1964, in *Brain and Conscious Experience*, ed. John Eccles (New York: Springer, 1966), p. 307.

15. Roger Sperry, "An Objective Approach to Subjective Experience: Further Explanation of a Hypothesis," *Psychological Review* 77 (1970): 587.

16. Thomas Natsoulas, "Roger W. Sperry's Monist Interactionism," *The Journal of Mind and Behavior* 8, no. 1 (1987): 1–22.

17. Natsoulas does not, to be sure, agree with everything Sperry has written. He objects to Sperry's 1952 paper, which interprets consciousness as produced by the expectation to respond rather than by stimulation. Natsoulas maintains that subjective experience cannot be response-dependent because it does not seem to vary with the response: "the experienced color does not change as one alternately calls it 'red' or presses a button. Moreover, one often produces responses *with reference to* how one experiences the environment or one's body; the response varies depending on how one takes one's experience qualitatively to be." Sperry himself has ameliorated his 1952 position considerably and his subsequent papers treat consciousness as a more central phenomenon.

18. Roger Sperry, "Perception in the Absence of the Neocortical Commissures," in *Perception and its Disorders, Research Publications of the Association for Research in Nervous and Mental Disease* 48 (1970): 136.

19. W. B. Weimer, "A Conceptual Framework for Cognitive Psychology: Motor Theories of Mind," in *Perceiving, Acting, and Knowing,* ed. R. Shaw and J. Bransford (Hillsdale, N.J.: Erlbaum, 1977), pp. 267–311. Weimer's judgment of Sperry's work is found on p. 292, where he refers to Sperry's work of 1952, 1965, 1968, 1969, and 1976 (as reported by Natsoulas, "Sperry's Monist Interactionism," p. 10).

20. Roger Sperry, "Mind-Brain Interaction: Mentalism, Yes; Dualism, No," *Neuroscience* 5 (1980): 196.

21. Natsoulas, "Sperry's Monist Interactionism," p. 12.

22. Ibid., p. 19.

23. Charles Ripley, "Sperry's Concept of Consciousness," *Inquiry* 27

(1984): 399. Ripley also has a number of other favorable things to say about Sperry's work in the same paper. He emphasizes that his careful examination of the language Sperry uses is not a result of a "natural love of picking nits," but, rather, was undertaken to prevent the misinterpretation "of a theory that I think to be extremely important" (p. 415). As well, Ripley sees Sperry's emphasis on how *micro-properties* and *macro-properties* can differ greatly in their nature and characteristics to be well taken. Dualists have often pointed to the tremendous difference between the nature of consciousness and that of other physical objects and systems which we are familiar with as evidence that "the mental and the physical must be entirely disparate forms of being." Sperry, Ripley notes with approval, "sees no force" in such a position (pp. 417–18).

24. Ripley, "Sperry's Concept of Consciousness," p. 419.
25. To provide the best explanation of the special kind of causality involved in the whole-part relationship, Ripley relies on Mario Bunge, whom he recomends as having given a "clear and viable account of such matters." (See Mario Bunge, *Treatise on Basic Philosophy*, vol. 3 [Dordrecht: Reidel, 1977].) Ripley, moreover, discovers the essential identity of Bunge's theories with Sperry's, while Bunge—who misinterprets his position—distances himself from Sperry's views. Ripley explains Bunge's misinterpretation through Sperry's lack of exactitude, but wonders whether Sperry has read Bunge. Yes, he did—as soon as Bunge was published—but found that he had expressed the same ideas ten years earlier.

The only real difference between Sperry and Bunge is that the latter conceives holistic causation (the determination of the fate of parts through the wholes they produced) as well as its counterpart (the determination of holistic properties by the constituents of that whole) as distinguishable from "external" causation, which (according to Bunge) is the only real cause-effect relationship. (Bunge's concept of noncausal determination is, however, not generally accepted in philosophy.)

26. Ripley, "Sperry's Concept of Consciousness" p. 419.
27. Roger Sperry, personal communication, 1985.
28. William Rottschaefer, "Roger Sperry's Science of Values," *The Journal of Mind and Behavior* 8, no. 1 (1987): 34.
29. Ibid.

30. Howard Slaatte, *The Creativity of Consciousness* (Lanham, N.Y.: The University Press of America, 1983).
31. Ibid.
32. Ibid., pp. 24, 25.
33. Colwyn Trevarthen, "Editor's Preface: Roger W. Sperry's Lifework and Our Tribute," in *Brain Circuits and Functions of the Mind: Essays in Honor of Roger W. Sperry* (New York: Cambridge University Press, 1990), p. xxxiii.
34. Ralph Lewis, "Most Important Theory in Decades," *The State News*, 19 October 1981, p. 4.
35. Ripley, "Sperry's Concept of Consciousness," pp. 399, 420.
36. David Hubel, "Introductory Comments," in *Two Hemispheres—One Brain: Functions of the Corpus Callosum*, ed. F. Lepore, M. Ptito, and H. H. Jasper (New York: Alan R. Liss, 1986), p. 169.
37. This compilation is based on library research for Roger Sperry's paper "Structure and Significance of the Consciousness Revolution," *The Journal of Mind and Behavior*, 8, no. 1 (1987): 37–65. Clearly the roots of the consciousness revolution would provide fertile ground for a historian of science to till; and a popular work on the area would surely have as wide an appeal as current studies of the making of modern physics.
38. Sperry, "The Consciousness Revolution," p. 37.
39. Gerald Edelman, *The Remembered Present* (New York: Basic Books, 1989), p. 254.
40. Natsoulas, "Sperry's Monist Interactionism"; Ripley, "Sperry's Concept of Consciousness."

Chapter 9. Toward Right-Hemisphere Acceptance

1. Roger Sperry, "Changed Concepts of Brain and Consciousness: Some Value Implications," lecture as part of the 1982/83 Isthmus Foundation Lecture Series in Science and Religion, in the Perkins School of Theology's *Perkins Journal* 36, no. 4 (1983): 21–32. Reprinted in *Zygon* 20 (1985): 41–57.
2. Ibid., p. 30.
3. Carl Casebolt, *A Polaris for the Spirit* (published by Concern for the Fulfillment of Life Foundation, 8041 Hansom Dr., Oakland, Calif. 94605, 1982).
4. Sperry, "Changed Concepts of Brain and Consciousness," *Zygon* reprint, p. 55.

5. CBC Radio Halifax, 29 August 1983.

6. *The New Columbia Encyclopedia*, 4th ed., s.v.. "plague"; *The Universal Standard Encyclopedia*, s.v. "plague, pestilence, or pest." Nicole Duplaix, "Fleas, the Lethal Leapers," *National Geographic* 173, no. 5 (1988): 672–94.

7. Frank Sommers (Physicians for Social Responsibility), "Medical and Psychological Effects of Nuclear War," paper presented at the Encounter Canada: War, Peace, and Canadian Security Conference, Toronto, 3–5 March 1983, *Peace Research Abstracts Journal* (December 1983): 24.

8. Lynn Margulis, "Symbiosis and the Evolution of the Cell," *Yearbook of the Science of the Future* (Chicago: Encyclopaedia Britannica, 1982): 104–121.

9. Thoughts like these caused Sperry to choose the title *Mind over Matter* for a forthcoming book describing his theory of consciousness—the theory that gives highest priority to human insights. Because the expression is commonly identified with dualism, however, Sperry later decided to change the title.

10. The distinction from social Darwinism is most clearly expressed in Sperry's paper "Changed Concepts of Brain and Consciousness," see e.g. p. 28.

11. Roger Sperry, "The New Mentalist Paradigm and Ultimate Concern," *Perspectives in Biology and Medicine* 29, no. 3 (1986): 419.

12. Garrett Hardin, *Stalking the Wild Taboo* (Los Altos, Calif.: William Kaufmann, 1973). This book provides a graph illustrating different levels of competition, moving from death (through stagnation) at one extreme to death (through too much competition and destruction of the environment) at the other with a desirable level somewhere intermediate (p. 175).

13. Bernard Davis, "The Importance of Human Individuality for Sociobiology," *Zygon* 15 (1980): 292.

14. This discussion on contrasting interpretations of Sperry's Grand Design of Nature is based on a ten-minute talk by Erika Erdmann to Sperry's psychobiology class during her first year of her work with Dr. Sperry (2 March 1982). Such a talk was demanded of every student as proof of his or her intelligent grasp of the subject matter.

15. The talk mentioned in note 14 contained a fuller version of the

quotation from William T. Jones's *The Sciences and the Humanities* (Berkeley and Los Angeles: University of California Press, 1965):

> This experience is not universal (like Hunger), but extremely valuable to those who encounter it; they want nothing else and nothing more. They experience a new certainty, confidence, and joy—together with a massive discharge of energy and realistic optimism.
>
> It is difficult to conceive of a more valuable character than one in which keen and realistic awareness of the complexities of life is combined with a refusal to despair and a readiness to act vigorously, cheerfully, and decisively.

16. Charles Birch and John B. Cobb, Jr., *The Liberation of Life* (New York: Cambridge University Press, 1981).
17. Jeremy Hayward, letter of 25 May 1990. (Cited with permission of the author.)
18. Jeremy Hayward, *Shifting Worlds, Changing Minds* (Boston: New Science Library/Shambhala, 1987).
19. Ibid., p. 282.
20. The Dalai Lama's official Nobel Lecture, "given by the Nobel Peace Prize Laureate 1989 HH Tenzin Gyatso, the 14. Dalai Lama, Oslo, December 11, 1989" (The Nobel Foundation, Stockholm), does not contain the quote cited from his original address of 10 October 1989.
21. Dalai Lama, *World Press Review* 37, no. 1 (January 1990): 64 (quoting from *l'Expres Paris*).

Chapter 10. Beyond a World Divided

1. Martin Luther King, Jr., as quoted in Carl Casebolt and Steve Rauh, *Toward Organic Security*, Special paper of the Peace and Environment Platform Project (World Citizens Assembly, Suite 506, 312 Sutter St., San Francisco, Calif. 94108, 1986).
2. Richard Thompson, *Foundations of Physiological Psychology* (New York: Harper & Row, 1967); and Peter Milner, *Physiological Psychology* (New York: Holt, Rinehart & Winston, 1970).
3. Sperry defends his position on the grounds that criticism leads to the advance of science. He subscribes to the conviction of the philosopher of science Karl Popper that only what is criticized will be changed, what is praised will stay the same.
4. Konrad Lorenz, *Behind the Mirror* (New York: Harcourt Brace Jovanovich, 1977), pp. 240–41.

5. Leon Kass, "Modern Science and Ethics," *University of Chicago Magazine* (Summer 1984), p. 30.

6. Erika Erdmann, *In Search of Values for Human Survival* (Ann Arbor, Mich.: University Microfilms International, 1987); and Erika Erdmann, *Challenge to Humanity: Values for Survival and Progress* Peace Research Reviews Vol. 11 no's. 3 and 4 (Dundas, Ont.: Peace Research Institute, 1989).

7. Roger Sperry, "Changed Concepts of Brain and Consciousness: Some Value Implications," lecture as part of the 1982/83 Isthmus Foundation Lecture Series in Science and Religion, in the Perkins School of Theology's *Perkins Journal* 36, no. 4 (1983): 21–32. Reprinted in *Zygon* 20 (1985): 28.

8. Peter Russell, *The Awakening Earth* (London: Ark Paperbacks/Routledge & Kegan Paul, 1984).

9. Erdmann, *Values for Human Survival*; and Erdmann, *Challenge to Humanity*.

Index

Mind-brain theories, 60

Monod, Jacques, 11, 13, 14, 16–17, 21, 22, 27, 28, 37, 39, 40, 76, 87, 97, 102, 104, 108, 120, 158, 175

Moral theory, Roman Catholic Church and, 25–26

Morgan, C. Lloyd, 116

Mumford, Lewis, 96

Natsoulas, Thomas, 142
  defense of Sperry's work, 133–37
  disagreement with Sperry, 198n.
  functional view of consciousness held by, 133

Newton, Isaac, 51

Nuclear war, effects of, 164

Optimal control systems, 127–28

Overpopulation, effects of, 73

Panpsychism, 105–06

Paradigms, Kuhn's concept of, 54

Pascal, Blaise, 94

Peacocke, Arthur, 12, 106, 108, 109

Penfield, Wilder, 142

Plague, effects of, 162–63

Polanyi, Michael, 94, 148

Pope, Alexander, 91, 94, 99

Popper, Karl, 75, 148, 159

Process theology, 170

Psychoneural isomorphism, 42

Psychophysical identity theory, and Sperry's philosophy, 140

Putnam, Hilary, 148

Reductionism, 11ff., 129ff.

Relational properties, 129–30

Religion, and science, 19ff., 75, 178
  and Sperry's ethics, 68–69

Resonance principle, 36

Ripley, Charles, 133, 137–40, 145, 147, 199n.

Rogers, Carl, 148

Rottschaeffer, William A., 144

Saint Matthews Island, 73

Salk, Jonas, 90, 98, 102, 173

Schaeffer, Francis, 4, 26–27, 28

Science, achievements of, 9–10
  contrasted with religion, 10
  objectives of, 18, 22

Self-consciousness, 21

Senses, limits of, 17–18

Simpson, George Gaylord, 111

Skinner, B. F., 52, 146

Slaatte, Howard A., on Sperry's philosophy, 144–46
  views on consciousness, 145–46

Smart, John, 52

Smith, Adam, 99

Snow, C. P., 3, 55, 98

Sociobiology, 22

Space-time factors, 117ff.

Spencer, Herbert, 165

Sperry, Roger W., 30, 31, 37, 38, 41, 42, 47, 49, 50, 51, 53, 54, 59, 64, 85, 98, 137, 146, 147, 156, 170, 177
  awards won by, 37, 39, 40, 189n.
  chemoaffinity theory of, 35–36, 37
  cognitive revolution, central factors in defined by, 149
  consciousness, theory of, 43, 56–58, 150
  Dialogues on Brain and Consciousness Conference, ideas discussed at, 197n.
  dualism, views on, 114
  early career of, 34–35
  emergence, views on, 121–22
  emergent causation, theory of, 50, 59–60
  emergent causation and modern physics, views on, 124
  Erdmann's personal view of, 181–82
  ethical system of, 69, 110–13
  ethical theory and mind-brain theory related, 66ff.
  ethical theory linked to emergent causation, 123